T0320401

Offensive and Defensive Cyber Security Strategies

The aim of this book is to explore the definitions and fundamentals of offensive security versus defensive security and describe the different tools and technologies for protecting against cyber threats. The book offers strategies of practical aspects of cybersecurity, covers the main disciplines needed to understand cybersecurity, and demonstrates ethical and legal concepts of cyber activities. It presents important concepts relevant for cybersecurity strategies, including the concept of cybercrime, cyber defense, protection of IT systems, and analysis of risks.

Dr. Mariya Ouaissa is currently Assistant Professor in Cybersecurity and Networks at the Faculty of Sciences Semlalia, Cadi Ayyad University, Marrakech, Morocco. She received her Ph.D. in 2019 in computer science and networks from Moulay Ismail University, Meknes, Morocco. She is a Networks and Telecoms Engineer and graduated in 2013 from the National School of Applied Sciences, Khouribga, Morocco. She has served and continues to serve on technical program and organizer committees of several conferences and events and has organized many symposiums/workshops/conferences as General Chair and also as a reviewer of numerous international journals. Dr. Ouaissa has made contributions in the fields of information security and privacy, Internet of Things security, and wireless and constrained networks security. She has published over 70 papers (book chapters, international journals, and conferences/workshops), 20 edited books, and 8 special issues as guest editor.

Dr. Mariyam Ouaissa is currently Assistant Professor of Networks and Systems at ENSA, Chouaib Doukkali University, El Jadida, Morocco. She received her Ph.D. degree in 2019 from the National Graduate School of Arts and Crafts, Meknes, Morocco, and her engineering degree in 2013 from the National School of Applied Sciences, Khouribga, Morocco. Dr. Ouaissa's research is multidisciplinary and focuses on the Internet of Things, M2M, WSN, vehicular communications and cellular networks, security networks, congestion overload problems, and the resource allocation management and access control. She has published more than 50 research papers (including book chapters, peer-reviewed journal articles, and peer-reviewed conference manuscripts), 15 edited books, and 6 special issues as guest editor. She has served on program committees and organizing committees of several conferences and events and has organized many symposiums/workshops/conferences as General Chair and TPC Chair.

Cyber Shorts Series

Discover concise and focused books on specific cybersecurity topics with Cyber Shorts. This book series is designed for students, professionals, and enthusiasts seeking to explore specialized areas within cybersecurity. From blockchain to zero-day to ethical hacking, each book provides real-world examples and practical insights.

Ransomware
Penetration Testing and Contingency Planning
Ravindra Das

Deploying the Zero Trust Framework in MSFT Azure
Ravindra Das

Generative AI
Phishing and Cybersecurity Metrics
Ravindra Das

A Reference Manual for Data Privacy Laws and Cyber Frameworks
Ravindra Das

Offensive and Defensive Cyber Security Strategies
Fundamentals, Theory and Practices
Mariya Ouaissa and Mariyam Ouaissa

For more information about this series, please visit: www.routledge.com/Cyber-Shorts/book-series/CYBSH

Offensive and Defensive Cyber Security Strategies
Fundamentals, Theory and Practices

Mariya Ouaissa and Mariyam Ouaissa

CRC Press
Taylor & Francis Group
Boca Raton London New York

CRC Press is an imprint of the
Taylor & Francis Group, an **informa** business

Designed cover image: © Shutterstock

First edition published 2025
by CRC Press
2385 NW Executive Center Drive, Suite 320, Boca Raton FL 33431

and by CRC Press
4 Park Square, Milton Park, Abingdon, Oxon, OX14 4RN

CRC Press is an imprint of Taylor & Francis Group, LLC

© 2025 Mariya Ouaissa and Mariyam Ouaissa

ISBN: 9781032823416 (hbk)
ISBN: 9781032833804 (pbk)
ISBN: 9781003509080 (ebk)

DOI: 10.1201/9781003509080

Typeset in Sabon LT Pro
by Apex CoVantage, LLC

Contents

Preface

Cybersecurity has become a critical issue for businesses, organizations, and individuals in today's digital age. With the increasing reliance on technology and the Internet, it is essential to have efficient measures in place to protect systems and networks from cyber threats. There are two main approaches to cybersecurity: offensive security and defensive security. Offensive security refers to the practice of actively attacking and exploiting computer systems and networks to test their defenses and identify vulnerabilities. Defensive security, on the other hand, refers to protecting computer systems and networks from attack by identifying and mitigating vulnerabilities and implementing measures to prevent or detect unauthorized access or activity.

In cybersecurity, strategies are broadly divided into two categories: offensive and defensive. While both approaches are vital, they offer different perspectives on protecting, detecting, and responding to threats. The key is employing the right strategy at the right time in order to protect against attackers, maintain business continuity in the face of cyberattacks, optimize resources, and adhere to regulatory compliance.

Offensive cybersecurity, commonly called "OffSec," focuses on actively seeking out systems' vulnerabilities, flaws, and weaknesses before attackers can exploit them. The premise behind OffSec is simple: to best defend oneself, one must think and act like an attacker. This proactive approach includes strategies like penetration testing (or pentesting), red teaming, phishing simulations, and vulnerability assessments. While offensive cybersecurity aims to identify vulnerabilities by actively simulating cyberattacks, defensive cybersecurity, or "DefSec," focuses on building and maintaining resilient systems that can prevent, detect, and respond to threats as they arise. This approach emphasizes layers of protection, including firewalls, antivirus software, intrusion detection systems (IDS), intrusion prevention systems (IPS), and incident response teams. The primary goal is to prevent, detect, and mitigate threats.

The aim of this book is to explore the definitions and fundamentals of offensive security and defensive security, and we will also consider the different tools and technologies for protecting against cyber threats.

The book offers strategies of practical aspects of cybersecurity and covers the main disciplines needed to understand cybersecurity. This book also demonstrates ethical and legal concepts of cyber activities.

The book presents important concepts relevant for cybersecurity strategies, including the concept of cybercrime, cyber defense, protection of IT systems, and analysis of risks.

Let us take a closer look at the specific themes and contributions of each chapter:

- The first and foundational chapter, Chapter 1, provides an overview of cybersecurity concepts and fundamentals, the main challenges in different components of infrastructure, cybersecurity frameworks, and regulations.
- Chapter 2 examines the evolution of offensive cybersecurity tools and technologies in the contemporary digital landscape by exploring the methods and means used by malicious actors to compromise system.
- In Chapter 3, we delve into the essential tools and technologies of defensive cybersecurity, aiming at shielding digital assets from cyber threats and attacks. The chapter provides a detailed examination of various defense mechanisms, such as intrusion detection systems, intrusion prevention systems, firewalls, antivirus software, encryption tools, and endpoint security solutions.
- Chapter 4 conducts a comprehensive overview of threat modeling and risk management in cybersecurity. Integrating threat modeling and risk management is essential for a robust security strategy. By combining these two practices, organizations can not only identify and assess potential threats but also proactively manage risks, ensuring stronger protection of their assets and information.
- Chapter 5 covers strategies and techniques for managing cybersecurity incidents and conducting digital investigations. It includes the essential steps of incident response. Additionally, it explores digital forensic methods for collecting, analyzing, and preserving electronic evidence, ensuring its integrity for use in forensic investigations.
- The final chapter, Chapter 6, presents the real-world applications, challenges, and future prospects of the convergence of AI, IoT, and blockchain for robust and adaptable cybersecurity in the face of evolving threats.

Each chapter serves as a piece of the larger puzzle, contributing valuable insights, innovations, techniques, and tools to the complex landscape of cybersecurity. We invite you to journey through this book, exploring the cutting-edge developments, challenges, and promising possibilities that await.

About the authors

Dr. Mariya Ouaissa is currently Assistant Professor in Cybersecurity and Networks at the Faculty of Sciences Semlalia, Cadi Ayyad University, Marrakech, Morocco. She received her Ph.D. in 2019 in computer science and networks at the Laboratory of Modelisation of Mathematics and Computer Science from the ENSAM-Moulay Ismail University, Meknes, Morocco. She is a Networks and Telecoms Engineer and graduated in 2013 from the National School of Applied Sciences, Khouribga, Morocco. She is a co-founder and IT consultant at the IT Support and Consulting Center. She was working for the School of Technology of in Meknes, Morocco, as a visiting professor from 2013 to 2021. She is a member of the International Association of Engineers and the International Association of Online Engineering, and, since 2021, she has been an "ACM Professional Member." She is Expert Reviewer with the Academic Exchange Information Centre (AEIC) and Brand Ambassador with Bentham Science. She has served and continues to serve on technical program and organizer committees of several conferences and events and has organized many symposiums/workshops/conferences as General Chair and also as a reviewer of numerous international journals. Dr. Ouaissa has made contributions in the fields of information security and privacy, Internet of Things security, and wireless and constrained networks security. Her main research topics are IoT, M2M, D2D, WSN, cellular networks, and vehicular networks. She has published over 50 papers (book chapters, international journals, and conferences/workshops), 15 edited books, and 8 special issues as guest editor.

Dr. Mariyam Ouaissa is currently Assistant Professor of Networks and Systems at ENSA, Chouaib Doukkali University, El Jadida, Morocco. She received her Ph.D. degree in 2019 from the National Graduate School of Arts and Crafts, Meknes, Morocco, and her engineering degree in 2013 from the National School of Applied Sciences, Khouribga, Morocco. She is a communication and networking researcher and practitioner with industry and academic experience. Dr. Ouaissa's research is multidisciplinary and focuses on the Internet of Things, M2M, WSN, vehicular communications and cellular networks, security networks, congestion overload problems, and the resource allocation management and access control. She is serving as a reviewer for international journals and conferences, including *IEEE Access* and *Wireless Communications and Mobile Computing*. Since 2020, she has been a member of the "International Association of Engineers IAENG" and the "International Association of Online Engineering," and since 2021, she has been an "ACM Professional Member." She has published more than 50 research papers (including book chapters, peer-reviewed journal articles, and peer-reviewed conference manuscripts), 13 edited books, and 6 special issues as guest editor. She has served on program committees and organizing committees of several conferences and events and has organized many symposiums/workshops/conferences as General Chair and TPC Chair.

Chapter 1

Fundamentals of cybersecurity strategies

1.1 INTRODUCTION

Today, the world is more interconnected than ever. The global economy relies on people's ability to communicate across time zones and access crucial information from anywhere. Cybersecurity enhances productivity and innovation by providing the confidence needed to work and communicate online securely [1].

Cybersecurity encompasses all measures that ensure the protection and integrity of data, whether sensitive or not, within a digital infrastructure. It involves a set of processes, best practices, and technology solutions that help protect critical systems and networks from digital attacks. Capitalizing on the surge in data and the growing number of people working and connecting remotely, malicious actors have devised sophisticated methods to access resources, steal data, sabotage businesses, and extort money. The number of attacks rises each year, with adversaries continuously developing new techniques to avoid detection. An effective cybersecurity program integrates people, processes, and technology solutions to mitigate the risk of business interruption, financial loss, and reputational damage in the event of an attack [2].

Individuals and organizations face different types of digital threats every day. These threats can include computer attacks or acts of espionage aimed at stealing personal data, targeted attacks to gain economic advantage, or cyberterrorism intended to create insecurity and distrust in large groups. A cyberattack refers to an action designed to target a computer or any element of a computerized information system (IS) with the aim of modifying, destroying, or stealing data, as well as exploiting or harming a network. It includes any type of offensive action that targets computer systems, infrastructure, networks, or even personal computers, using various methods to steal, modify, or destroy data or systems [3].

This chapter offers a thorough analysis of the fundamentals of cybersecurity, focusing particularly on technical cyberattacks. The aim is to provide a comprehensive overview of cybersecurity and the principal frameworks and

DOI: 10.1201/9781003509080-1

regulations used in different scenarios. The structure of this chapter is organized as follows. Section 1.2 provides a description of technical cyberattacks.
Section 1.3 presents the anatomy of a cyberattack. Sections 1.4 and 1.5
describe the fundamentals and frameworks of cybersecurity. In Section 1.6,
we discuss implementing cybersecurity measures. Compliance and regulations are covered in Section 1.7. Finally, Sections 1.8 and 1.9 present the
main professions and future trends in cybersecurity, respectively. Conclusions are drawn in Section 1.10.

1.2 UNDERSTANDING CYBER THREATS

Cyberattacks have seen a significant increase in recent years due to techno-
logical advancements and the digitalization of almost all areas of social life.
The advent of teleworking, e-commerce, cloud computing, and other online
activities has greatly expanded the attack surface. Indeed, computer systems
present numerous vulnerabilities that can be exploited by hackers, whether
at the network, software, or infrastructure level. A cyberattack occurs when
a malicious actor exploits weakness in a computer system, network, or software. These attacks can take various forms, such as denial of service (DoS),
espionage, data destruction, ransomware, and phishing. Cyberattacks pose
the greatest threat to any institution or individual in a highly digitalized
world, as they target all sectors of society, including governments, the private
sector, as well as civil and military organizations. In this section, we focus
on identifying the most common types and techniques of cyberattacks [4].

1.2.1 Malware

Malware consists of computer programs designed to disrupt the normal
operation of a system or cause damage to data. The purpose of malware is
determined by its malicious intent, acting against the victim's requirements
for the system. These types of software have become tools for both hackers
and governments to steal personal, financial, or business data. Malware can
encrypt or delete sensitive data, modify or hijack functions, spy on victim
activity, or even generate money. Additionally, it can be used for sabotage or
politically motivated purposes. There are various types of malware, including spyware, ransomware, and others [5].

1.2.1.1 Virus

The virus infiltrates applications such as Microsoft Word or Excel by embedding itself into the application's initialization sequence. Upon opening the
application, the virus executes its instructions before relinquishing control to

the application. Subsequently, the virus duplicates itself and affixes to other codes within the computer system.

1.2.1.2 Trojan horses

This program hides inside seemingly useful software and usually performs malicious functions. Unlike other viruses, Trojan does not replicate itself. In addition to launching attacks against a system, Trojan can establish a back-door that attackers can exploit. For example, Trojan can be programmed to open a high-numbered port for a hacker to listen in and then execute an attack.

1.2.1.3 Drive-by download attack

This attack entails the discreet insertion of a malicious script into a website's code. When users visit the site, a covert download is initiated automatically. Drive-by download attacks are a prevalent technique for distributing malware. Hackers target vulnerable websites and embed a malicious script into the HTTP or PHP code of a page. This script can either install malware directly onto the visitor's computer or redirect the visitor to a site controlled by the hackers.

1.2.1.4 Logic bomb

This type of malware is added to an application and triggered by a specific event, such as a logical condition or a specific date and time.

1.2.1.5 Worms

Unlike viruses, worms do not rely on attaching to host files; they are stand-alone programs capable of spreading autonomously across networks and computers. Typically transmitted through email attachments, worms commonly exploit the method of sending copies of themselves to each email contact stored on the infected computer. In addition to carrying out nefarious actions, worms spreading across the Internet and overwhelming mail servers can instigate DoS attacks against network nodes.

1.2.1.6 Ransomware

This type of malware restricts access to the victim's data and threatens to publish or delete it unless a ransom is paid. While basic ransomware may lock the system in a way that a knowledgeable person can easily fix, more advanced ransomware employs a technique called "crypto-viral extortion."

This method encrypts the victim's files, making them nearly impossible to recover without the decryption key. With ransomware, the victim's system is effectively held hostage until the ransom is paid to the attacker. After the payment is made, the attacker provides instructions on how the victim can regain control of their computer [6].

1.2.1.7 Adware

These software applications are used by businesses for marketing purposes. Advertising banners are displayed while a program is running. Adware may be automatically downloaded to your system when you browse a website and may appear in pop-up windows or in a bar that automatically appears on your computer screen.

1.2.1.8 Spyware

These programs are installed to gather information about users, their computers, or their browsing habits. They monitor activities without the user's knowledge and send the data to a remote operator. Additionally, they can download and install other malicious programs from the Internet. While spyware functions similarly to adware, it is typically a separate program that installs covertly when a free application is installed. This spyware collects and transmits personal information without the user's knowledge or consent.

1.2.2 DoS attack

DoS attack aims to inundate a system's resources to the extent that it becomes incapable of responding to legitimate service requests. Similarly, a Distributed Denial of Service (DDoS) attack operates with the intention of depleting a system's resources. However, a DDoS attack occurs when a large number of host machines are infected with malware and controlled by the attacker [7]. These machines, called "botnets," simultaneously flood the target with illegitimate requests, overwhelming its resources. With a DoS attack, the target site is saturated with illegitimate requests. Since the site must respond to every request, its resources are consumed by all the responses, rendering it incapable of serving legitimate users. This often results in the site shutting down completely (Figure 1.1).

1.2.2.1 TCP SYN flood attack

In this assault, the attacker takes advantage of buffer space usage during the TCP session initiation handshake. By inundating the target system's processing queue with connection requests from their own machine, the attacker

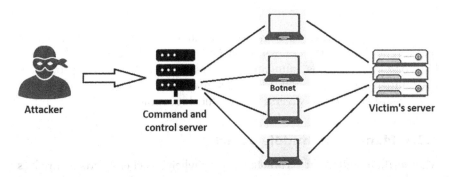

Figure 1.1 DDoS attack

does not respond when the target attempts to establish connections. Consequently, the target system times out while awaiting a response, potentially resulting in a crash or rendering it unusable due to the congested connection queue.

1.2.2.2 Teardrop attack

This type of attack induces overlapping of the length and fragmentation offset fields within consecutive Internet Protocol (IP) packets at the targeted host. As the targeted system endeavors to reconstruct the packets, it encounters failure and confusion, ultimately leading to a crash.

1.2.2.3 Smurf attack

In this attack, the perpetrator falsifies an IP address and utilizes Internet Control Message Protocol (ICMP) to inundate a designated network with traffic, often by directing ICMP echo requests toward broadcast IP addresses. To mitigate this attack, IP-directed broadcasts to routers should be disabled to intercept ICMP echo requests at network devices. Alternatively, endpoints can be configured to refrain from responding to ICMP packets originating from broadcast addresses.

1.2.2.4 Ping of death

This offensive tactic involves pinging a target system with IP packets surpassing the maximum size of 65,535 bytes. The attacker fragments these packets, and upon reassembly by the target system, it may encounter buffer overflows and crashes. Firewalls equipped to verify the maximum size of fragmented IP packets can thwart ping of death attacks.

1.2.2.5 Botnets

Botnets are vast networks composed of millions of systems infected with malware and under the control of hackers to execute DDoS attacks. These bots, or zombie systems, inundate target systems' bandwidth and processing capabilities. The origin of DDoS attacks from botnets is arduous to trace due to their dispersal across diverse geographical locations.

1.2.3 Man-in-the-middle attack

Man-in-the-middle (MitM) attack happens when a hacker inserts themselves into the communication between a client and a server (Figure 1.2). Here are some common types of MitM attacks [8].

1.2.3.1 Session hijacking

In this attack, an attacker takes over a session between a trusted client and a network server. The attacker's computer replaces the trusted client's IP address with its own, and the server continues the session, thinking it is still communicating with the client.

1.2.3.2 IP spoofing

An attacker uses IP spoofing to trick a system into believing it is communicating with a known and trusted entity. The attacker sends a packet to the target host that contains the source IP address of a known and trusted host instead of their own.

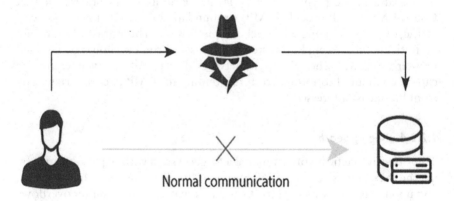

Normal communication

Figure 1.2 MitM attack

1.2.3.3 Replay attack

This attack occurs when an attacker intercepts and saves old messages, and then resends them, pretending to be one of the participants. Techniques such as session time stamps or nonces can counter this type of attack.

1.2.4 Phishing attack

Phishing involves sending emails that appear to originate from trusted sources with the goal of obtaining personal information or tricking users into taking specific actions. This technique combines social engineering and technical tactics. It may involve an email attachment that installs malware on your computer or a link to a fraudulent website that tricks you into downloading malware or disclosing personal information [9]. To carry out the cyberattack, the attacker might send a link that redirects you to a deceptive website, where you unknowingly download malware such as viruses, or it might enable the attacker to access your private information. Often, the victim remains unaware of the compromise, allowing the attacker to contact others within the same organization without raising suspicion of malicious activity.

1.2.4.1 Whale-phishing attack

Whale-phishing attacks are named so because they target the "big fish" or "whales" of an organization, typically senior executives, senior management, or others at a high level within the organization. These individuals often possess valuable information sought by attackers, such as proprietary company information or operational details [10].

1.2.4.2 Spear-phishing attack

Spear phishing refers to a specific type of more targeted phishing attack. Attackers invest time in researching their targets and craft messages that are likely to be relevant to them. These cyberattacks are aptly named "spear" phishing due to the focused approach on specific targets. The messages appear legitimate, making it challenging to detect a spear-phishing attack [11].

1.2.5 Password attack

Because passwords serve as the primary method to authenticate users of a computer system, acquiring passwords constitutes a common and effective attack strategy. Passwords can be obtained through various methods, such as searching a person's physical desktop, monitoring network connections to intercept unencrypted passwords, employing social engineering techniques, accessing password databases, or utilizing guessing. The guessing method can involve random attempts or systematic approaches.

1.2.5.1 Brute force attack

This involves trying different passwords in the hopes that one will work. Some logic can be applied, such as trying passwords related to the person's name, job title, hobbies, or other personal information.

1.2.5.2 Dictionary attack

This method involves using a list of common passwords to try to gain access to a user's computer and network. One technique is to obtain an encrypted file containing passwords, apply the same encryption to a dictionary of commonly used passwords, and then compare the results to see if any match.

1.2.6 Eavesdropping attack

Eavesdropping attacks involve the attacker intercepting traffic as it traverses the network. In doing so, the attacker can capture sensitive information such as usernames, passwords, and credit card details. Eavesdropping can take on two forms: active or passive. During active eavesdropping, the hacker inserts software into the network traffic's path to collect and analyze information, allowing them to extract useful data. In contrast, passive eavesdropping involves the hacker simply monitoring transmissions, seeking valuable data to exploit, without altering the traffic.

1.2.7 Birthday attack

In a birthday attack, an attacker exploits a security feature: hashing algorithms used for verifying the authenticity of messages. A hash algorithm acts as a digital signature that the message recipient verifies to confirm the message's authenticity. If a hacker can generate a hash identical to the one attached by the sender, they can replace the sender's message with their own. The receiving device will accept it because it matches the correct hash. Birthday attacks target hashing algorithms that verify message integrity, software, or digital signatures.

1.2.8 Cross-site scripting attack

In a cross-site scripting (XSS) attack, the attacker distributes malicious scripts via clickable content sent to the victim's browser. When the victim clicks on the content, the script is activated. Since the user is already logged into a web application, the input they provide is considered valid by the application. However, the executed script has been tampered with by the attacker, resulting in unintended actions being performed on behalf of the user.

1.2.9 Structured Query Language injection attack

Structured Query Language (SQL) injection is a prevalent method for exploiting websites that rely on databases to serve their users. Clients, which are devices retrieving information from servers, instigate an SQL attack by dispatching an SQL query to a server's database. In this attack, the command is "injected" into a data plane instead of the expected input, such as a password or username.

1.2.10 Zero-day attack

These attacks exploit recently discovered but unpatched vulnerabilities to carry out their malicious tasks. Various detection mechanisms have been proposed to protect against these attacks; yet they remain prevalent and pose significant challenges in cybersecurity.

1.3 ANATOMY OF A CYBERATTACK

Most attacks adhere to the pattern illustrated in Figure 1.3.

Figure 1.3 Steps of an anatomy of a cyberattack

1.3.1 Cyber scanning

Network reconnaissance is a crucial step in all organized attacks. It serves as the initial stage in an intrusion attempt, enabling an attacker to collect extensive information about the target and identify vulnerable systems for remote exploitation.

1.3.2 Enumeration

It involves testing discovered vulnerabilities to identify weak points that allow attackers to gain access to the system.

1.3.3 Intrusion attempt

The cybercriminal can infiltrate the network or employ advanced attacks to render it unusable.

1.3.4 Elevation du privilege

According to the Microsoft STRIDE model, escalation of privilege occurs when a malicious user gains a higher level of authorization than is typically assigned to them.

1.3.5 Perform malicious tasks

These tasks involve damaging or stealing data.

1.3.6 Deploy malware/backdoor

The cybercriminal installs malware on the target endpoint device to create a backdoor, enabling the downloading of multiple types of malware. This facilitates various attacks to be carried out efficiently.

1.3.7 Delete forensic evidence and exit

This final step involves attackers removing all traces of their presence from the network and systems. They frequently utilize viruses and worms to eliminate potentially incriminating evidence.

1.4 FUNDAMENTALS OF CYBERSECURITY

1.4.1 Confidentiality, integrity, and availability triad

Cybersecurity encompasses a range of practices, technologies, measures, and processes designed to safeguard sensitive data, networks, and critical systems from digital threats like unauthorized intrusions and disruptive interruptions. Its primary objective is to ensure the confidentiality, integrity, and availability (CIA) of data and IS through diverse defense mechanisms against cyberattacks (Figure 1.4) [12].

- **Confidentiality**: Confidentiality involves implementing data protection measures to ensure that data remains accessible only to authorized individuals and is not misused. The stringency of these measures may vary depending on the sensitivity of the data and the potential damage from unauthorized access by malicious actors.
- **Integrity**: Integrity ensures the consistency, accuracy, and reliability of data from creation to deletion. This includes measures to prevent unauthorized modifications during transmission.
- **Availability**: Availability means that authorized users can access data whenever necessary, requiring measures to maintain a functional operating environment.

The CIA triad forms the foundation of cybersecurity. Breaches or attacks compromise one or more of these principles. Additionally, cybersecurity includes other essential characteristics:

- **Non-repudiation**: Non-repudiation preserves transaction integrity and trust in system operations, utilizing mechanisms such as action traceability, electronic signatures, or audit logs to prevent users from

Figure 1.4 CIA triad

disputing legitimate transactions. For instance, a student who submits an exam on the Moodle platform cannot later deny doing so.

- **Authentication**: Authentication is crucial for identifying users and managing their access to appropriate workspaces, thereby ensuring IS security. A robust security strategy with multiple layers of protection against malicious online activity is essential for effective cybersecurity.

1.4.2 Principle of least privilege

The principle of least privilege is a cybersecurity concept that entails granting users just enough access to the network and IS necessary to perform their duties, without providing unnecessary privileges. This principle is vital because granting excessive privileges increases the company's attack surface and facilitates lateral movement for attackers in the event of a breach. The main benefits of the principle of least privilege include:

- **Reduced attack surface**: Limiting user privileges minimizes potential avenues for attackers to exploit systems and data.
- **Prevention of lateral movement**: By adhering to the principle of least privilege, malicious actors are restricted to the systems and data accessible to compromised credentials, preventing lateral movement within the network. This limitation reduces the risk of malware dissemination and data exfiltration.
- **Mitigation of insider threats**: Restricting access according to the principle of least privilege helps mitigate insider threats stemming from malicious actions, errors, or negligence by company employees. For instance, limiting application installation to system administrators prevents end users from inadvertently or intentionally installing malware.
- **Strengthening compliance**: Least privilege access aids in enforcing compliance with industry and regulatory standards such as the Health Insurance Portability and Accountability Act (HIPAA) and General Data Protection Regulation (GDPR) by restricting user access to sensitive data.

1.4.3 Encryption and its role in cybersecurity

Cryptography, a fundamental component of IT security, plays a crucial role in safeguarding communications and data from malicious attacks. Operating on encryption keys, cryptography ensures the confidentiality, integrity, and authenticity of data across networks and IS. It involves the use of encryption algorithms to convert sensitive information into secret codes, rendering it inaccessible to unauthorized individuals. This protection against cyber threats relies on encryption algorithms that generate cryptographic keys, ensuring the confidentiality of data whether it is in transit or at rest. Only with a decryption key can encrypted data be deciphered. Cryptography employs cryptographic algorithms that utilize mathematical functions to encrypt and decrypt data using keys such as phrases or numbers. The security of cryptography hinges on the robustness of the algorithms and the confidentiality level of the key employed. While complex combinations of cryptographic algorithms and keys enhance cryptography's effectiveness, they also necessitate additional computational resources. Various types of cryptography, including symmetric cryptography, asymmetric cryptography, and hash functions, are employed to encrypt communications and data.

- **Symmetric or secret key cryptography**
  - It utilizes a single cryptographic key for both encryption and decryption of data.
  - The size of the encrypted text remains the same as or smaller than the plaintext.
  - It requires a secure mechanism for the transmission of the decryption key between parties.
- **Asymmetric or public key cryptography**
  - It employs distinct public and private key pairs for secure communication.
  - The ciphertext size is the same as or larger than the plaintext.
  - Communication is encrypted using the public key and decrypted using the private key.
  - It offers higher security compared to symmetric cryptography but is notably slower.
- **Hash function**
  - It utilizes a hash function to convert plaintext into a fixed-size hash value.
  - The output size of the hash function is fixed, regardless of the message length.
  - It ensures message integrity; if the message remains unaltered, the hash values on both ends will match.
  - It does not involve the use of public or private keys.

Additionally, cryptography involving elliptic curves, or elliptic curve cryptography, employs mathematically advanced techniques. While offering heightened security, it is also more resource-intensive and time-consuming compared to asymmetric encryption methods.

1.5 CYBERSECURITY FRAMEWORKS

Cybersecurity frameworks offer a solid foundation for formulating your cyber strategy and enhancing your security maturity [13].

1.5.1 National Institute of Standards and Technology cybersecurity framework

Originating from the United States, the National Institute of Standards and Technology (NIST) cybersecurity framework was initially designed for private sector organizations but has gained widespread adoption by governments worldwide. NIST offers a comprehensive framework for preventing, detecting, and responding to a variety of common cyberattacks. It consists of standards, guidelines, and best practices aimed at managing IT risks. As such, it serves as a methodological framework that companies can choose to follow voluntarily without legal obligation. The framework aids in anticipating security breaches and managing and reducing identified IT risks. It is structured around three main components: core, implementation levels, and profiles, each of which guides the assessment of cybersecurity risk management's impact on the organization's operational and financial performance.

- **Core:** The core formulates the organization's risk management strategy, focusing on five primary functions: identify, protect, detect, respond, and recover. These functions are subdivided into categories and subcategories and supplemented with informative references or documentary resources.
- **Implementation levels:** These levels enable the evaluation of the company's existing cyber risk management processes, supporting the assessment of the organization's maturity in this area. The assessment categorizes maturity into four levels: partial, informed, repeatable, or adaptive risk management.
- **Profile:** The profile outlines how the organization manages its cyber risks in alignment with its strategic objectives. Comparing the current profile to the target profile helps identify priority actions to be implemented.

1.5.2 ISO/IEC 27001

To establish a comprehensive framework for information security, the International Organization for Standardization (ISO) and the International Electrotechnical Commission (IEC) have developed the ISO 27000 series of standards. These standards delineate a management approach for IT risks, encompassing a set of processes related to IS management. The primary objective is to assist organizations in safeguarding their data, which may include financial records, customer information, strategic data, trade secrets, intellectual property, and more.

The ISO/IEC 27000 family of standards is applicable to businesses of all sizes and across various sectors. Among the standards within this family, ISO/IEC 27001 stands out as the most recognized. This standard, along with numerous others in the series, outlines requirements for Information Security Management Systems (ISMS). Implementing standards from this family streamlines the management of security for sensitive assets such as financial data, intellectual property records, employee information, and data entrusted by third parties.

1.5.3 Center for Internet Security controls

Developed by the Center for Internet Security (CIS), the CIS Critical Security Controls comprise a structured and systematic collection of cybersecurity's best practices and defensive measures. These controls are designed to mitigate the most prevalent and severe cyber threats while promoting compliance across various regulatory frameworks. Crafted by a consortium of IT professionals, these best practices are informed by real-world attack data and successful defense strategies. The CIS controls offer precise recommendations and a well-defined roadmap for organizations to adhere to, enabling them to meet the requirements outlined by numerous legal, regulatory, and policy frameworks.

1.5.4 MITRE ATT&CK

A bit distinct from the others on this list, MITRE ATT&CK functions more as a knowledge repository than a rigid framework. Rooted in practical experience, it furnishes a collection of matrices containing insights into prevalent attack tactics and mitigation strategies. Users can delve into any aspect of the cyber kill chain or explore specific adversary tactics and techniques, allowing for the creation of personalized approaches tailored to their organization's needs.

1.5.5 Control Objectives for Information and Related Technologies

Control Objectives for Information and Related Technologies (COBIT) is a well-established framework developed by information systems audit and control association (ISACA). This framework encompasses all critical processes essential for efficient IT management. While it serves as a valuable overall resource, the latest iteration, COBIT 5, underscores information security, especially in navigating evolving enterprise landscapes influenced by factors like Bring Your Own Device (BYOD) and remote work practices.

1.6 IMPLEMENTING CYBERSECURITY MEASURES

1.6.1 Network security

Network security encompasses the tools, technologies, and processes utilized to safeguard a company's network and critical infrastructure from unauthorized access, cyberattacks, data breaches, and other security risks. A comprehensive network security strategy aims to prevent, detect, contain, and mitigate various cyber threats by leveraging advanced technologies and human expertise. This strategy encompasses protective measures for all hardware systems, software applications, and endpoints, as well as the network itself, including network traffic, data, and both physical- and cloud-based data centers. Network security relies on three key components: protection, detection, and response.

- **Protection:** This entails proactive security measures taken by an organization to thwart cyberattacks and malicious activities. It may involve employing tools such as next-generation antivirus (NGAV) or implementing rules such as privileged access management (PAM).
- **Detection:** Detection involves the capability to analyze network traffic, identify potential threats, and promptly respond to them. Advanced endpoint detection and response (EDR) solutions typically provide these capabilities. EDR tools use sophisticated data analysis techniques to monitor and record network activities, detect suspicious system behavior, and offer contextual information and remediation recommendations to cybersecurity professionals.
- **Response:** Response pertains to the organization's ability to swiftly address security incidents. This often involves utilizing a managed detection and response (MDR) system, which combines technology and human intelligence to conduct threat hunting, monitoring, and response activities. Additionally, an effective response may include implementing a formal incident response plan outlining the steps required to prevent, detect, mitigate, and recover from data breaches or security events.

1.6.2 Endpoint security

Endpoint security involves securing the endpoints of computer networks, which encompass electronic devices like PCs, laptops, smartphones, or tablets. In cybersecurity, endpoints are considered the frontline defense. Endpoint security systems aim to safeguard network entry points or cloud environments from a range of cybersecurity threats. Initially, these systems comprised traditional antivirus software, but modern tools now provide robust protection against advanced malware and security vulnerabilities. These contemporary systems are engineered to detect, analyze, block, and contain ongoing attacks. Collaboration among these systems and other security technologies is crucial for administrators to gain visibility into threats and expedite detection and response processes.

1.6.3 Application security

AppSec involves identifying, mitigating, and preventing security vulnerabilities at the application level within software development processes. This encompasses integrating application security metrics throughout the development life cycle, spanning from planning to production deployment. Previously, security was often addressed post-application design and development. However, there is a shift toward incorporating security earlier in the development and testing phases. By embedding AppSec from the outset, organizations can significantly diminish the likelihood of security vulnerabilities in their code or in third-party components utilized in an application.

Web application security encompasses diverse processes, technologies, or methodologies aimed at safeguarding servers, applications, and web services like APIs from Internet-based attacks. It is vital for shielding data, customers, and organizations from data breaches, disruptions in business continuity, or other adverse outcomes of cyber threats. A significant portion of cybercrime targets applications and their vulnerabilities, estimated at over three-quarters. Web application security strategies utilize measures such as web application firewalls (WAF), multifactor authentication (MFA), safeguarding and validating cookies to maintain user state integrity and confidentiality, and various techniques for validating user input to ensure it is non-malicious before processing by an application.

Numerous security threats pose risks to software applications. However, the Open Web Application Security Project's (OWASP) Top Ten list of application threats consolidates the most prevalent and severe threats likely to impact applications in production. AppSec initiatives should prioritize addressing these high-profile threats prevalent in modern applications:

- **Injection:** Code injection involves sending a request or command to a software application containing malicious or untrusted data. The most common form is SQL injection, but it can also affect NoSQL servers, operating systems, and LDAP servers.
- **Weak authentication:** Many application sites feature inadequate or flawed authentication and authorization mechanisms, enabling attackers to steal user credentials or gain unauthorized access.

- **Exposure of sensitive data:** Applications and APIs may inadvertently expose sensitive organizational or customer data, including financial information, payment data, and personally identifiable information (PII).
- **XML external entities (XXE):** Attackers exploit legacy XML parsers by maliciously referencing external entities in XML documents to access internal files, scan ports, and remotely execute code.
- **Inadequate access control:** Insufficiently implemented restrictions on authenticated users enable attackers to access unauthorized functions or data, compromise user accounts, access sensitive files, or modify user permissions.
- **Misconfigured security:** Security features may be improperly configured, often due to unchanged default application settings or the absence of updates to operating systems and frameworks.
- **Cross-site scripting:** XSS enables attackers to execute malicious scripts in users' browsers, potentially leading to session hijacking, redirection to malicious sites, or website defacement.
- **Insecure deserialization:** Flaws in code extraction from files and transformation into objects can facilitate malicious code execution, privilege escalation, and replay attacks by authorized users.
- **Use of components with known vulnerabilities:** Several vulnerability databases catalog known vulnerabilities in software components. Applications using vulnerable components, even as dependencies, are susceptible to attacks.
- **Insufficient logging and monitoring:** Many application sites lack adequate mechanisms to identify or record attempted breaches, allowing breaches to go undetected and enabling attackers to pivot to compromise other systems.

1.6.4 Cloud security

Cloud security encompasses a set of procedures and technologies designed to mitigate external and internal threats to business security. As organizations embark on their digital transformation journey and incorporate cloud-based tools and services into their infrastructure, securing the cloud becomes imperative. Terms like "digital transformation" and "cloud migration" have become commonplace in business vocabulary, signifying the shift toward modern technologies. While these technologies offer flexibility and scalability, transitioning to predominantly cloud-based environments requires careful consideration of security implications. The three primary cloud computing services are as follows:

- **Infrastructure-as-a-Service (IaaS):** This hybrid solution allows organizations to manage some data and applications on-premises while

leveraging cloud computing providers for managing servers, hardware, network, virtualization, and storage needs.
- **Platform-as-a-Service (PaaS):** PaaS streamlines application development and delivery by offering a customizable application canvas that automatically manages operating systems, software updates, cloud storage, and supporting infrastructure.
- **Software-as-a-Service (SaaS):** SaaS delivers cloud-based software hosted online, typically on a subscription basis. Third-party providers handle technical aspects like data, middleware, servers, and storage, reducing IT resource expenses and simplifying maintenance and support functions.

The dynamic nature of infrastructure management, particularly in scaling applications and services, presents challenges for businesses in adequately resourcing their services. As-a-service models enable businesses to offload time-consuming IT-related tasks. However, security threats have evolved to become more sophisticated, targeting cloud computing providers due to organizations' limited visibility into data access and movement. Failure to enhance cloud security can expose organizations to significant governance and compliance risks associated with managing customer information, irrespective of its storage location.

1.6.5 Mobile security

The future of computing and communication is increasingly centered around mobile devices, such as laptops, tablets, and smartphones, which offer desktop-like functionality in a portable form factor. Their compact size, diverse operating systems, extensive application ecosystems, and robust processing power make them indispensable tools that can be utilized virtually from anywhere with an Internet connection. Moreover, with the proliferation of rugged devices, the Internet of Things (IoT), and operating systems like Chrome OS, macOS, Windows 10, and Windows 11, virtually every hardware device equipped with these software platforms and features becomes inherently mobile.

As mobile devices have become more affordable and portable, both businesses and individual users are gravitating toward them instead of relying solely on traditional desktop computers. However, the widespread availability of Wi-Fi access renders all types of mobile devices susceptible to various forms of cyberattacks and data breaches.

While authentication and authorization via mobile devices offer unparalleled convenience, they also introduce additional risks by circumventing the constraints imposed by a secure corporate perimeter. New features alter the landscape of user authentication and local authorization for both the device itself and the applications and services accessed over the network.

Consequently, these advancements significantly expand the number of endpoints that must be safeguarded against cybersecurity threats.

Phishing remains the predominant security threat in the mobile domain, involving fraudulent attempts to steal user credentials or sensitive data, such as credit card numbers. Cybercriminals employ deceptive tactics, such as sending bogus emails or SMS messages masquerading as legitimate sources, complete with fake hyperlinks. Meanwhile, mobile malware represents another insidious menace, comprising stealthy software entities like malicious applications or spyware designed to wreak havoc, disrupt operations, or gain unauthorized access to clients, computers, servers, or entire computer networks. Ransomware, a particularly pernicious form of malware, leverages encryption to hold a victim's data or files hostage until a ransom is paid, ostensibly to decrypt the files and restore access.

However, the evolving landscape of mobile security presents both new challenges and opportunities, necessitating a fundamental reevaluation of security paradigms for personal computing devices. IT and security teams must reassess how to effectively address security requirements in light of evolving device capabilities, the ever-changing mobile threat landscape, and shifting user expectations.

1.7 COMPLIANCE AND REGULATIONS

1.7.1 Common Vulnerability Scoring System

Common Vulnerabilities and Exposures (CVE) serves as a comprehensive catalog of publicly known security vulnerabilities, aiding cybersecurity professionals in assessing and addressing potential threats. Utilizing the Common Vulnerability Scoring System (CVSS), CVE assigns scores to vulnerabilities based on standardized criteria, enabling professionals to gauge their severity accurately. Managed by the MITRE Corporation, the CVE Glossary Project is dedicated to diligently monitoring and documenting information security vulnerabilities, with support from the U.S. Department of Homeland Security (DHS). The CVSS employs three key metrics—basic, temporal, and environmental—to evaluate vulnerabilities objectively. The resulting score, ranging from 0 to 10, provides a clear indication of the criticality of each vulnerability, facilitating prioritization and mitigation efforts.

1.7.2 General Data Protection Regulation

GDPR stands as the cornerstone legislation for data protection at the European level. This regulation was officially published in May 2016 following several years of development. Notably, as a European regulation rather than a directive, the GDPR took immediate effect across all member states of the European Union without the need for individual transpositions. The primary objectives of the GDPR are twofold: to bolster the protection of individuals whose personal data is processed and to enhance the accountability of entities engaged in such processing activities. These fundamental principles are intended to be enforced with greater efficacy through the heightened authority granted to supervisory bodies.

1.7.3 Health Insurance Portability and Accountability Act

HIPAA comprises a set of U.S. federal regulatory standards delineating the lawful use and disclosure of protected health information within the United States. Oversight of HIPAA compliance falls under the jurisdiction of the Department of Health and Human Services (HHS) and is enforced by the Office for Civil Rights (OCR). Compliance with HIPAA represents an ongoing commitment and cultural shift that healthcare organizations must embed within their operations to safeguard the privacy, security, and integrity of protected health information. Enacted to govern the handling and security of health information, HIPAA mandates stringent security controls for electronic health information and establishes privacy practices. The law applies to two primary categories of entities: "covered entities," such as healthcare providers, health plans, and health information clearinghouses, as well as their corporate affiliates, including billing companies, Electronic Health Record (EHR) vendors, consultants, and IT service providers.

1.7.4 Payment Card Industry Data Security Standard

The Payment Card Industry Data Security Standard (PCI DSS) is a standard applicable to all entities involved in the electronic payment ecosystem, including those that process, transmit, or store cardholder data. PCI DSS aims to safeguard end users as well as all entities within the payment chain by preventing the theft of sensitive banking information through a comprehensive set of rigorous standards. Compliance with PCI DSS is crucial for protecting users, intermediaries, banks, and merchants alike. In many cases, adherence to PCI DSS standards is mandatory for businesses to conduct transactions with major card issuers such as Visa, Mastercard, JCB, Discover, and American Express. Therefore, it is imperative for organizations to establish and uphold a robust data security policy that includes regular vulnerability assessments and penetration testing to ensure ongoing compliance with PCI DSS requirements [14].

1.8 CYBERSECURITY PROFESSIONS

Cybersecurity professionals evaluate the security of computer systems and networks to identify vulnerabilities and address them effectively. Their role is critical in safeguarding businesses and organizations against cyberattacks.

1.8.1 SOC analyst

This configures security monitoring systems (SIEM, probes, honeypots, and filtering equipment); categorizes, analyzes, and processes security alerts regularly to enhance their effectiveness; and ensures detection, investigation, and response to security incidents. The SOC analyst analyzes and interprets alerts, correlated events, and searches for vulnerabilities.

1.8.2 Technical auditor

The primary mission of a technical security auditor is to verify that a company's IT systems are secure and protected against various IT threats. IT systems assess the security measures in place on a given system to detect vulnerabilities and weaknesses in terms of security.

1.8.3 Pentester

A pentester is responsible for testing systems to detect weaknesses. It simulates attacks as it would be carried out by cyberattackers (e.g., to steal data or compromise a system) and proposes action plans to correct the flaws.

1.8.4 DevSecOps consultant

The term "DevOps" corresponds to the blend of tasks performed by a company's teams responsible for application Development (Dev) and system Operations (Ops). DevSecOps aims to integrate security at every stage of the DevOps cycle. Therefore, we have the continuous DevOps cycle strengthened by security.

1.8.5 Chief Information Security Officer

Chief Information Security Officer (CISO) is responsible for the security of IS and manages the entire security department. It is a crucial position, often requiring direct communication with the IT department or even the company's CEO. However, in the event of a major security incident, the CISO could also be the first person held accountable.

1.9 FUTURE TRENDS IN CYBERSECURITY

1.9.1 Artificial intelligence in cybersecurity

Artificial intelligence (AI) enables the continuous processing of large volumes of data, aiding in the detection of new security risks. AI algorithms learn over time, reducing the need for repetitive procedures and enhancing cybersecurity capabilities. AI also alleviates humans from time-consuming tasks, reducing the risk of human error, a significant contributor to cyber-security risks. These advantages are particularly beneficial for incident and threat management processes. Threat management involves collecting vast amounts of information about threats and operationalizing it to better counter attacks. This requires relevant and structured information to provide a timely and appropriate response to malware. AI helps manage information overload by processing data quickly and efficiently. In incident response, AI plays an increasingly important role. This process involves several stages, including incident analysis, restoration planning, and implementation. Many tasks within this process can be partially automated with AI, such as antivirus reinstallation, registry key checks, and firewall rule modifications. Penetration tests aim to identify vulnerabilities within the IS for exploitation. Given the extensive range of possible vulnerabilities, human capacity alone may not be sufficient. AI, with its machine learning (ML) capabilities, emerges as a potential support for addressing these vulnerabilities effectively [15].

1.9.2 Zero trust security model

Zero trust is a cybersecurity strategy where security policies are enforced based on contextual factors established through least privilege access controls and strict user authentication, rather than relying on implicit trust. A well-implemented zero trust architecture streamlines network infrastructure, enhances user experience, and bolsters defense against cyber threats. This approach follows the principle of "never trust, always verify," which was introduced by John Kindervag during his tenure at Forrester Research. In a zero trust architecture, access policies are determined by various contextual elements, such as user roles, device status, and requested data, to prevent unauthorized access and lateral movement within an environment. Implementing a zero trust architecture necessitates robust visibility and control over users and traffic within the environment, including encrypted traffic. Organizations must monitor and verify traffic between different parts of the environment and deploy strong MFA methods, such as biometrics or one-time codes, to augment security beyond simple passwords. In a zero trust architecture, the network location of a resource loses its prominence as the primary security factor. Instead, software-defined microsegmentation is employed to safeguard data, workflows, services, and other assets, allowing organizations to protect them anywhere, whether in traditional data centers or distributed hybrid and multicloud environments.

1.9.3 IoT security challenges

IoT encompasses all physical objects capable of connecting to the Internet. This expansive category includes a growing array of devices such as personal assistants, connected children's toys, surveillance cameras, smart bulbs, sensors, shutters, blinds, gates, switches, connected sockets for smart homes, and health monitoring wearables like smartwatches. IoT has gained significant attention among the general public due to innovations such as wearable fitness trackers, autonomous vehicles, and smart home technologies. However, its influence extends across various sectors, including industry, through concepts like Industry 4.0 and ongoing innovation. These connected devices are increasingly penetrating sensitive domains such as energy distribution, healthcare, pharmaceuticals, aerospace, and transportation, among others [16].

1.10 CONCLUSION

The increasing integration of computing technologies into the workplace has brought numerous benefits to the business ecosystem. However, it has also exposed organizations to heightened risks of cybercrime. Cybersecurity has emerged as a critical discipline aimed at safeguarding the CIA of information in this digital landscape. Effective cybersecurity measures must span the entire life cycle of data, from its creation and processing to its transmission, storage, and disposal, ensuring that it is managed securely at every stage. As cybercriminals continue to exploit vulnerabilities in IS, the importance of robust cybersecurity practices cannot be overstated. This chapter has provided an overview of key cybersecurity concepts, challenges across various infrastructure components, relevant frameworks, and regulatory considerations. Moreover, it has outlined the essential roles played by cybersecurity professionals and highlighted emerging trends shaping the future of cybersecurity. As organizations navigate the evolving threat landscape, prioritizing cybersecurity initiatives remains paramount to safeguarding digital assets and maintaining trust in the digital age.

REFERENCES

[1] K. S. Wilson, and M. A. Kiy, "Some fundamental cybersecurity concepts," IEEE Access, vol. 2, 2014, pp. 116–124.
[2] H. Taherdoost, "Cybersecurity vs. information security," Procedia Computer Science, vol. 215, 2022, pp. 483–487.
[3] M. Ouaissa, and M. Ouaissa, "Cyber security issues for IoT based smart grid infrastructure," IOP Conference Series: Materials Science and Engineering, vol. 937, no. 1, 2020, p. 012001.
[4] Y. Li, and Q. Liu, "A comprehensive review study of cyber-attacks and cyber security; Emerging trends and recent developments," Energy Reports, vol. 7, 2021, pp. 8176–8186.
[5] A. Bendovschi, "Cyber-attacks–trends, patterns and security countermeasures," Procedia Economics and Finance, vol. 28, 2015, pp. 24–31.

[6]   M. F. Safitra, M. Lubis, and H. Fakhrurroja, "Counterattacking cyber threats: A framework for the future of cybersecurity," Sustainability, vol. 15, no. 18, 2023, p. 13369.

[7]   M. K. Hasan, A. A. Habib, S. Islam, N. Safie, S. N. H. S. Abdullah, and B. Pandey, "DDoS: Distributed denial of service attack in communication standard vulnerabilities in smart grid applications and cyber security with recent developments," Energy Reports, vol. 9, 2023, pp. 1318–1326.

[8]   D. Javeed, U. Mohammed Badamasi, C. O. Ndubuisi, F. Soomro, and M. Asif, "Man in the middle attacks: Analysis, motivation and prevention," International Journal of Computer Networks and Communications Security, vol. 8, no. 7, 2020, pp. 52–58.

[9]   Z. Alkhalil, C. Hewage, L. Nawaf, and I. Khan, "Phishing attacks: A recent comprehensive study and a new anatomy," Frontiers in Computer Science, vol. 3, 2021, p. 563060.

[10] B. Naqvi, K. Perova, A. Farooq, I. Makhdoom, S. Oyedeji, and J. Porras, "Mitigation strategies against the phishing attacks: A systematic literature review," Computers & Security, 2023, p. 103387.

[11] G. A. Thomopoulos, D. P. Lyras, and C. A. Fidas, "A systematic review and research challenges on phishing cyberattacks from an electroencephalography and gaze-based perspective," Personal and Ubiquitous Computing, 2024, pp. 1–22.

[12] C. P. Pfleeger, "The fundamentals of information security," IEEE Software, vol. 14, no. 1, 1997, pp. 15–16.

[13] H. Taherdoost, "Understanding cybersecurity frameworks and information security standards—a review and comprehensive overview," Electronics, vol. 11, no. 14, 2022, p. 2181.

[14] H. Zafar, "Human resource information systems: Information security concerns for organizations," Human Resource Management Review, vol. 23, no. 1, 2013, pp. 105–113.

[15] Z. Boulouard, M. Ouaissa, M. Ouaissa, M. Krichen, M. Almutiq, and K. Gasmi, "Detecting hateful and offensive speech in Arabic social media using transfer learning," Applied Sciences, vol. 12, no. 24, 2022, p. 12823.

[16] M. Ouaissa, A. Rhattoy, and I. Chana, "New security level of authentication and key agreement protocol for the IoT on LTE mobile networks," In 2018 6th International Conference on Wireless Networks and Mobile Communications (WINCOM), pp. 1–6. New York: IEEE, 2018.

Chapter 2

Offensive cybersecurity tools and technologies

2.1 INTRODUCTION

The cybersecurity field encompasses all efforts undertaken by businesses and security teams to safeguard their IT assets from attacks, covering both defensive and offensive tasks [1].

Offensive security entails employing the same tools, tactics, and techniques as real attackers to test an organization's defenses. However, rather than causing harm, security teams leverage these methods to enhance the organization's security posture. It is a proactive, adversarial approach aimed at shielding computer systems, networks, and individuals from attacks. Defensive security, on the other hand, focuses on identifying and, in some cases, disrupting attackers, emphasizing reactive measures like software patching and vulnerability remediation [2].

In the ongoing battle against cyber threats, defenders engage in a constant cat-and-mouse game with cybercriminals and other threat actors. As attackers innovate, defenders respond with countermeasures, prompting attackers to find ways to circumvent these defenses. Relying solely on defensive measures means that an organization's security tools and defenses are only truly tested during an actual attack. Moreover, developing new defenses occurs in isolation, often without a clear understanding of the gaps that need to be addressed in the organization's defenses [3].

This chapter examines the evolution of offensive cybersecurity tools and technologies in today's cyberspace context. By exploring the methods and means malicious actors use to compromise system security, it highlights the growing importance of developing effective countermeasures. The analysis covers a range of techniques, such as social engineering, sophisticated malware, DDoS attacks, and reverse engineering. By highlighting the challenges and ethical questions associated with using these tools, this chapter aims to provide cybersecurity practitioners with information on best practices for protecting digital infrastructures against persistent and emerging threats. This chapter is organized into the following sections. In Section 2.2, we propose an overview of offensive cybersecurity. Section 2.3 presents the

DOI: 10.1201/9781003509080-2

offensive cybersecurity techniques and tactics. Section 2.4 describes the offensive cybersecurity tools. We conclude in Section 2.5.

2.2 UNDERSTANDING OFFENSIVE CYBERSECURITY

2.2.1 Overview of offensive versus defensive cybersecurity

Defensive cybersecurity comprises an organization's measures to shield itself from attacks, including deploying security solutions, establishing security protocols, and training employees to detect phishing attempts. It involves both proactive steps to prevent cyberattacks and reactive actions to detect, block, and mitigate ongoing attacks [4].

In essence, offensive cybersecurity represents the threats that defensive cybersecurity aims to counter. Cybercriminals test, evade, and breach an organization's defenses to steal data or cause harm, whereas ethical hackers do the same to uncover vulnerabilities for remediation before malicious actors exploit them.

A robust cybersecurity strategy integrates both offensive and defensive measures. This approach enables organizations to defend against cyber threats effectively while leveraging offensive techniques to refine and strengthen their defenses continuously [5].

Offensive security employs a proactive, adversarial approach to safeguard computer systems, networks, and individuals from attacks, while defensive security focuses on identifying perpetrators and, if possible, disrupting their activities. Defensive efforts prioritize reactive actions like software patching and vulnerability remediation (Figure 2.1).

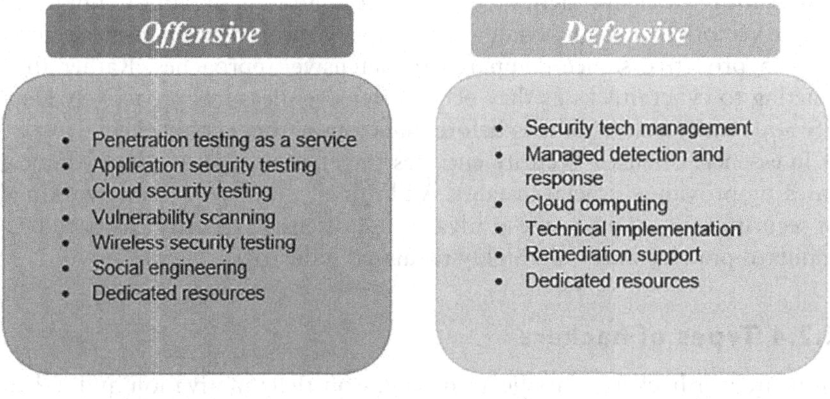

Offensive	**Defensive**
• Penetration testing as a service • Application security testing • Cloud security testing • Vulnerability scanning • Wireless security testing • Social engineering • Dedicated resources	• Security tech management • Managed detection and response • Cloud computing • Technical implementation • Remediation support • Dedicated resources

Figure 2.1 Overview of offensive versus defensive cybersecurity

2.2.2 Objectives of offensive cybersecurity

Offensive security encompasses proactive strategies that employ tactics similar to cybercriminals to strengthen network security rather than compromise it. Key offensive security techniques include red teaming, penetration testing, and vulnerability assessment.

These operations are typically conducted by ethical hackers, cybersecurity experts who leverage their skills to identify and remedy vulnerabilities in computer systems. Unlike malicious hackers, who exploit systems for data theft or malware deployment, ethical hackers operate with explicit permission to simulate breaches. Consequently, their actions result in no actual harm, and the insights gained from simulated attacks aid organizations in fortifying their defenses [6].

Historically, offensive security also involved strategies designed to thwart cybercriminals, such as setting traps or decoys to mislead attackers. However, these adversarial tactics are less prevalent in today's cybersecurity landscape.

2.2.3 Benefits of offensive cybersecurity

To grasp the significance of offensive security, it is beneficial to contrast it with defensive security.

Defensive security mechanisms, such as antivirus programs and firewalls, operate reactively. They aim to thwart known threats or identify suspicious activities. Advanced tools like security orchestration, automation, and response (SOAR) platforms can even automate responses to ongoing attacks. However, these defensive strategies often burden security teams. Analysts must sift through numerous alerts and data to discern genuine threats from false alarms. Moreover, defensive measures primarily address known attack vectors, leaving organizations susceptible to new or unidentified cyber threats.

Offensive security serves as a complement to defensive strategies. Security teams utilize offensive tactics to uncover and address previously unknown attack vectors that might evade other security measures. Offensive security takes a proactive stance compared to defensive approaches. Rather than reacting to cyberattacks as they occur, offensive measures proactively identify and rectify vulnerabilities before malicious actors exploit them.

In essence, offensive security enriches the effectiveness of defensive measures by providing crucial insights. Additionally, it alleviates the workload of security teams. Due to these advantages, offensive security has become a standard practice in certain highly regulated industries.

2.2.4 Types of hackers

Ultimately, a hacker's classification hinges on their motivation and adherence to legal boundaries [7] (Figure 2.2).

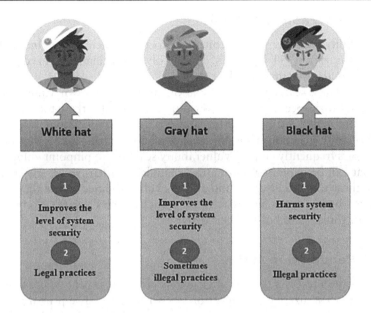

Figure 2.2 Types of hackers

- **White hats:** Well-intentioned hackers utilize their hacking talent to defend companies. They are IT security professionals, ethical hackers who operate within a well-defined legal framework to assess the security of an IS.
- **Gray hats:** They operate in a gray area of legality. They conduct tests and notify their targets of discovered vulnerabilities for correction with advance notice before disclosure.
- **Sponsored hackers:** In the age of cyberwar, some countries often enlist this group of hackers to attack another country, while others train their own elements if necessary.
- **Script kiddies:** They are not always trained and lack in-depth knowledge of security and law, typically rely on downloading tools from the Internet to conduct their tests.
- **Black hats:** Badly intentioned hackers are highly skilled but seek to cause harm. In the jargon, they are referred to as "crackers."

2.3 COMMON OFFENSIVE CYBERSECURITY TECHNIQUES AND TACTICS

Tactics, techniques, and procedures (TTPs) employed by offensive security professionals mirror those used by cybercriminals. By leveraging these TTPs, they can identify and address potential vulnerabilities that real hackers could exploit, thereby testing the efficacy of existing security programs [8].

2.3.1 Vulnerability analysis

Vulnerability scanning is an automated process for detecting vulnerabilities in an organization's IT resources. This involves utilizing specialized tools to scan computer systems for vulnerabilities.

Vulnerability scanners are capable of identifying known vulnerabilities associated with specific software versions. Additionally, these tools can conduct more active testing, such as observing how applications respond to common SQL injection strings or other malicious intrusions.

Hackers frequently employ vulnerability scanners to pinpoint vulnerabilities that can be exploited in an attack. Similarly, offensive security experts utilize these tools to discover and address vulnerabilities before they can be exploited by hackers. This proactive approach enables organizations to stay ahead of threats and bolster their defenses.

2.3.2 Penetration test

A penetration test is a type of offensive security assessment where a human evaluator scrutinizes an organization's cyber defenses. The primary goal of these assessments is to reveal as many vulnerabilities as possible within an organization's security infrastructure. Penetration test is crucial as it helps identify vulnerabilities that may go undetected by automatic scanners due to the human intelligence and expertise involved. Regular penetration test assists organizations in closing vulnerabilities that are most likely to be exploited by a human attacker.

Penetration test involves simulating cyberattacks to identify vulnerabilities in computer systems. Similar to vulnerability scanners, ethical hackers (or pentesters) conducting these tests simulate real hackers to uncover potential network vulnerabilities. By adopting the perspective of a cybercriminal, they can identify many vulnerabilities that are prime targets. Through penetration test, human security experts can detect vulnerabilities that might evade fully automated tools. As they exploit identified vulnerabilities, they are less likely to produce false positives. Moreover, if they can exploit a vulnerability, cybercriminals could potentially do the same. Additionally, because penetration test is often conducted by third-party security services, it tends to uncover vulnerabilities that internal security teams might overlook [9].

Penetration tests can be carried out internally (with some access to the company's IS) or externally (without access to the company's IS). These tests typically involve using a combination of automated and manual tools to assess business resources.

It is important to note that penetration test is distinct from both hacking and ethical hacking (Figure 2.3).

Penetration Test	Hacking	Ethical Hacking
• A well-defined framework • Follows testing methodologies • Is based on governance standards • Is carried out over a given period	• Objective of compromise • No defined framework • No methodology • Opportunistic search for vulnerabilities • Not constrained by time	• Well-intentioned objective • No defined framework • No methodology • Opportunistic search for vulnerabilities • Not constrained by time

Figure 2.3 Penetration test versus hacking versus ethical hacking

2.3.2.1 Black box, white box, and gray box

White box, black box, and gray box exercises are not distinct forms of assessment; rather, they delineate the level of knowledge and access granted to attackers. Each approach has its pros and cons [10]:

- White box: In a white box assessment, the assessor has full access to the company's systems and documentation, simulating an attack by an insider with considerable power, such as a system administrator. This extensive knowledge and access make it easier to target potential vulnerabilities, but testers may risk being influenced by documentation and focusing on intended system functionality rather than actual performance.
- Black box: In a black box evaluation, the tester operates with no prior knowledge or access, simulating an external attacker. Although this approach reduces bias, it may demand more time and resources for reconnaissance and attack planning.
- Gray box: Gray box assessment falls between white box and black box evaluations, granting the tester the same level of knowledge and access as a typical user. This approach strikes a balance between the advantages and drawbacks of both white box and black box methods.

These three approaches to offensive security testing can be applied across various testing forms. With greater knowledge and access, a penetration tester or red team member has more options compared to a black box assessment. Moreover, additional knowledge and access can influence the configuration and implementation of automated tools for vulnerability scanning.

2.3.2.2 Penetration test methodologies

OffSec teams also adhere to established ethical hacking methodologies, such as Open Source Security Testing Methodology Manual (OSSTMM), Penetration Testing Execution Standard (PTES), and OWASP.

- **OSSTMM methodology**: It offers a comprehensive approach to penetration testing, covering five channels: human security, physical security, wireless communications, telecommunications, and data networks. By assessing security across these channels, organizations gain insight into their overall security posture and evaluate the effectiveness of their security processes. OSSTMM employs modular concepts, defining sets of processes or phases applicable to each channel, tailored to real-world domains and technical and regulatory constraints.
- **PTES methodology:** It comprises seven main sections that encompass the entire penetration testing process. It starts with initial communication and reasoning, progresses through intelligence gathering and threat modeling, and continues to vulnerability research, exploitation, and post-exploitation phases. Finally, it culminates in reporting, which provides a coherent summary of the entire process, delivering maximum value to the customer.
- **OWASP methodology:** An international nonprofit organization, it focuses on enhancing software security. Its mission is to promote software security visibility and provides resources to improve application security. One core principle of OWASP is the free availability of their materials, including documentation, tools, videos, and forums. This accessibility empowers individuals and organizations to enhance the security of their software.

The materials offered by OWASP consist of community-initiated projects that undergo validation and promotion by the OWASP board following a structured roadmap.

Among the most renowned OWASP projects are:

- OWASP TOP 10: A document outlining the ten most critical security risks for web applications.
- OWASP ZAP: A web proxy tool designed for web application security testing.
- OWASP Web Security Testing Guide: A methodology for conducting penetration testing on web applications.
- OWASP Juice Shop: A deliberately vulnerable web application used for practicing web penetration testing and educating users.
- OWASP Amass: A tool utilized for mapping the attack surface and discovering external assets.

The OWASP methodology encompasses comprehensive guides for testing the security of web, mobile, and firmware applications. These guides, developed through collaboration among cybersecurity professionals and volunteers, offer a framework of best practices employed by penetration testers and organizations globally.

2.3.2.3 Red/blue/purple team

Red team exercises and penetration testing share the commonality of being conducted by humans rather than relying on fully automated processes. However, a significant distinction lies in their respective objectives: while red teaming missions assess an organization's defenses against specific threats, penetration testing is geared toward uncovering as many vulnerabilities as possible.

In contrast, blue and purple team exercises involve different parties and levels of collaboration. In a purple team exercise, there is heightened cooperation and knowledge exchange between the offensive red team and the defensive blue team.

Red team assessments strive to replicate real-world attacks, often targeting specific objectives like data breaches or ransomware delivery. Regular penetration testing helps organizations detect vulnerabilities that could be exploited by human attackers, enabling them to address these security shortcomings effectively.

2.3.2.4 Phases of penetration test process

A penetration test can be segmented into a series of steps or phases, forming a comprehensive methodology [11]. While these phases may vary in name and number, they provide a holistic overview of the penetration testing process. For simplicity, we will outline this procedure in four main phases:

1. Step 1: Reconnaissance
2. Step 2: Scanning (ports, vulnerabilities, etc.)
3. Step 3: Exploitation
4. Step 4: Post-exploitation and maintaining access

These steps, although subject to variation depending on methodologies, are supported by various tools.

2.3.2.4.1 Reconnaissance

The objective of the reconnaissance stage is to gather information about the target, enhancing the likelihood of success in subsequent steps. Information gathering predominantly leverages the Internet, employing both active and passive reconnaissance strategies.

Active reconnaissance involves direct interaction with the target, potentially exposing the attacker's IP address and actions to detection. Conversely, passive reconnaissance, or Open Source Intelligence (OSINT), relies on publicly available information without direct interaction.

Passive reconnaissance aims to gather information that illuminates or broadens the attack surface of the target. Various resources and tools are employed for information collection:

- Search engines
- Social networks
- Websites specializing in public information collection on organizations
- OSINT tools
- Social engineering techniques

2.3.2.4.2 Scanning

At the outset of this initial phase, regardless of the available data, our objective is to compile a list of IP addresses for scanning. The second step, scanning, is divided into two separate activities. The first activity entails port scanning, allowing us to compile a list of open ports and potential services operating on each target. The second activity involves vulnerability scanning, which aims to identify and locate specific weaknesses within the software and services running on the targets.

2.3.2.4.3 Exploitation

Next, we move on to the exploitation phase. With precise knowledge of the open ports on the target, the services running on these ports, and the associated vulnerabilities, we can launch an attack. This phase constitutes the actual "hacking." Exploitation can involve various techniques, tools, and code. The primary goal of exploitation is to gain administrator access (full control) over the target machine. This can occur locally or remotely. A local exploit requires the attacker to have physical access to the computer, while a remote exploit occurs across networks and systems when the attacker cannot physically touch the target. Through exploitation, programs can be installed, defense tools disabled, confidential documents copied, modified, or deleted, and security settings altered. Exploitation is the process of gaining partial or complete control over a system. More specifically, an exploit takes advantage of a security flaw or bypasses security controls to gain administrator-level access to the computer. In many cases, exploitation aims to transform the target machine into a "zombie" machine that follows the attacker's commands. An exploit is the realization, materialization, or weaponization of a vulnerability. Exploits are failures or bugs in software that allow the attacker to launch a payload on the target system.

2.3.2.4.4 Post-exploitation and maintaining access

The final step is post-exploitation and maintaining access. Often, the payloads delivered during the exploitation phase only provide temporary access to the system. Therefore, it is necessary to create a permanent backdoor on the system, ensuring administrator access that persists even after programs are closed or the computer is restarted. For a pentester, one of the most crucial activities of a penetration test is writing the report. Regardless of the time and effort invested in the penetration test, the client will often judge the quality and effectiveness of your work based on this written report. The report must include all relevant information discovered during the test, provide a detailed explanation of how the test was conducted, and describe the operations performed. Where possible, it should also present risk mitigation measures and solutions to the identified security issues. The report should offer a nontechnical overview of the findings in one or two pages, highlighting and briefly summarizing the critical issues identified by the test. It must be understandable to a broad audience.

2.3.3 Social engineering test

While several tests concentrate on breaching an organization's IT systems and circumventing digital defenses, it is crucial to acknowledge that many cyber threat actors exploit the human element in their attacks rather than solely targeting software vulnerabilities. Social engineering testing is designed to evaluate the effectiveness of employees, contractors, and other individuals within an organization in safeguarding its data and systems. Social engineers employ deception, manipulation, and similar tactics to deceive or coerce targets into carrying out actions that serve the attacker's interests. These actions may include divulging sensitive data or providing access to secure company sites or applications. Social engineering testing is instrumental in assessing an organization's resilience against such tactics and identifying areas for improvement in human-centric security measures.

2.3.4 Red teaming

Red teaming, or adversarial simulation, involves a group of experts using the TTP of real cybercriminals to launch a simulated attack against a computer system. Unlike penetration testing, red teaming assesses a company's security by pitting two teams against each other. The red team actively exploits attack

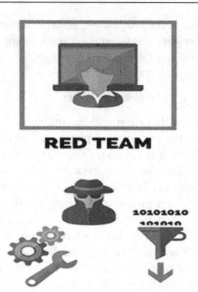

Figure 2.4 Red teaming

vectors (without causing actual damage) to see how far they can penetrate, while the blue team, composed of security engineers, is tasked with stopping them. This exercise allows the organization to concretely test its incident response procedures (Figure 2.4).

Organizations can establish an internal red team or hire a third party. To test both technical defenses and employee awareness, the red team may employ a range of tactics, including simulated phishing or ransomware attacks, social engineering exercises, and on-site breach techniques like tailgating.

Red teams can perform different types of tests depending on the amount of information they have:

1 **White box testing:** The red team has full transparency into the internal structure and source code of theA target system.
2 **Black box testing:** The red team has no prior information about the system and must breach it as real cybercriminals would.
3 **Gray box testing:** The red team has some basic information about the target system, such as IP address ranges for network devices.

2.3.5 Advanced persistent threats

An advanced persistent threat (APT) is a targeted, prolonged cyberattack in which an unauthorized individual gains access to the network and goes unnoticed for a significant period of time. The goal of an APT attack is typically to monitor network activity and steal data rather than damage the network or organization [12].

2.3.5.1 APT operating mode

Most state-sponsored attacks aim to compromise a company for espionage or sabotage over a long period, remaining undetected. The term "advanced persistent threat" is often misused. Rather than designating a specific technical approach taken in response to a threat, it describes the attacker (or group of attackers) and their underlying motivations, beyond simple espionage, financial gain, or one-off offenses. APTs are typically motivated by industrial espionage, aiming to steal valuable trade secrets and intellectual property, or by sabotaging an organization's plans and infrastructure [13] (Figure 2.5).

APT attackers use various messaging-based techniques to generate attacks, supported by physical and external exploitation techniques. Here are the characteristics specific to APT attacks not typically found in other forms of attacks:

- **Reconnaissance**: APT attackers leverage intelligence and reconnaissance to identify the users and systems that will help them achieve their goals. This information is often gleaned from social media, public forums, and intelligence from state security agencies.
- **Life cycle**: APT techniques are designed to evade detection for long periods, unlike attacks typically motivated by financial gain, which aim for brief system infections. APT attackers strive to leave no trace, often operating outside office hours. To re-access the system if their initial intrusion is detected, they always leave backdoors, ensuring persistence.
- **Advanced malware**: APT attackers exploit a wide range of known intrusion techniques and often combine multiple methodologies in a single attack. They use commercially available crime kits and software,

Figure 2.5 Operating mode of APT

but also have the technology and expertise to develop custom tools and polymorphic malware for specific environments and systems.

- **Phishing**: Many APTs begin with social engineering and spear phishing. After compromising a user's computer or stealing network login credentials, attackers deploy their tools to monitor and invade the network, moving from machine to machine and network to network, until they find the desired information.
- **Active attack**: Unlike traditional criminal attacks, APTs require strong involvement and coordination from the attackers, rather than relying on fully automatic malicious code. The adversary is a fully armed, motivated, and skilled attacker who is extremely active and highly targeted in their approach.

2.3.5.2 How does an APT attack?

Hackers who commit APT attacks take the following important steps to gain permanent access to the target network [14]:

- Network access: APT attackers initially reach their target systems through the Internet, often by sending targeted phishing messages or exploiting security vulnerabilities that allow them to introduce malware.
- Establish a foothold: Once they gain access, attackers dig deeper, using the installed malware to create backdoor networks and tunnels, allowing them to remain unnoticed. They may employ advanced malicious techniques such as code rewriting to cover their tracks.
- Spread the attack: After penetrating the target network, APT actors might hack administrative passwords, which grants them better control over the system and access to other levels.
- Move around the system: With administrative privileges, attackers can move laterally within the corporate network. They often attempt to access additional servers or other protected areas of the network.
- Deploy the attack: At this stage, attackers centralize, encrypt, and compress the data to facilitate exfiltration.
- Data exfiltration: Hackers collect the data and transmit it to their own systems.
- Maintaining undetected access: Cybercriminals can repeat this process over an extended period while remaining invisible. They may also create backdoors to regain access to the system whenever desired.

Unlike most common cyberattacks, APT campaigns use targeted methods rather than broad-spectrum tools designed to maximize the number of victims. APT campaigns tend to last longer than regular attacks because they are more strategic and covert, making them harder to detect and stop.

2.3.5.3 APT detection

Certain warning signs, though difficult to detect, may indicate the presence of an APT. Once a network is targeted, an organization may notice several symptoms [15]:

- **Unusual activity on user accounts:** Unexpected or atypical behaviors, such as login attempts at odd hours or from unusual locations, can be a red flag.
- **Unintentional use of a hijacked Trojan horse:** APTs often utilize Trojan horses to facilitate network access, which might manifest as unexpected software behaviors or system anomalies.
- **Variable or strange database activity:** This includes sudden increases in database transactions, particularly those involving large amounts of data, which could indicate data harvesting or preparation for exfiltration.
- **Presence of unusual data files:** This is the appearance of files that seem out of place or unexpected, suggesting that data might be compiled for extraction.
- **Anomaly detection in output data:** This is perhaps the most effective tool for detecting APT attacks. Unusual patterns or spikes in data output, especially those that do not align with normal business operations, can signal that data is being exfiltrated.

By closely monitoring these indicators, cybersecurity professionals can better identify and respond to potential APT activities, even though these signs may be subtle and challenging to detect.

2.4 OFFENSIVE CYBERSECURITY TOOLS

Working in offensive security requires experience in hacking, knowledge of programming languages, and familiarity with web application security. To validate their expertise, offensive security professionals often obtain certifications such as Offensive Security Certified Professional (OSCP) or Certified Ethical Hacker (CEH). These certifications demonstrate a solid understanding of penetration testing, ethical hacking principles, and security assessment techniques. Additionally, offensive security professionals are proficient in using common offensive security tools, including those given below [16].

2.4.1 Kali Linux

Kali Linux is a Debian-based open-source Linux distribution tailored for advanced penetration testing and security auditing. It offers a comprehensive suite of tools, numbering several hundred, to support various information security tasks, including penetration testing, security research, forensic analysis, and reverse engineering. This cross-platform solution is freely available to information security professionals and enthusiasts alike.

Designed specifically for professional penetration testing and security audits, Kali Linux comes preloaded with most OSINT tools such as reconng, theHarvester, SpiderFoot, and Maltego. Its architecture reflects the stringent requirements of these tasks through several key features:

- **Default network services disabled**: Kali Linux employs system hooks to deactivate network services by default, ensuring a secure environment regardless of installed packages. Even services like Bluetooth are initially blocked to maintain security.
- **Custom Linux kernel**: It utilizes a custom-patched upstream kernel optimized for wireless injection, a critical capability in penetration testing.
- **Minimal and reliable repositories**: Recognizing the paramount importance of system integrity, Kali Linux adheres to a minimal set of upstream software sources. This conservative approach safeguards against potential risks associated with adding additional repositories, which could compromise system stability.

By incorporating these fundamental changes and providing a rich repository of security tools, Kali Linux remains an indispensable resource for professionals engaged in penetration testing and security audits.

2.4.2 Network mapper (Nmap)

Nmap est un scanner de réseau utilisé pour découvrir les appareils connectés à un réseau, analyser les ports ouverts, et identifier les services en cours d'exécution sur ces ports. Considéré comme la norme de l'industrie des scanners, Nmap est un outil extrêmement puissant, amplifié par son moteur de scripts qui permet de rechercher des vulnérabilités et, dans certains cas, d'exécuter directement des exploits.

2.4.3 Nessus

Nessus is a vulnerability scanner that employs techniques akin to Nmap to identify and report vulnerabilities, presenting them in a user-friendly graphical user interface (GUI) interface. What sets Nessus apart from other scanners is its approach; it does not make assumptions during scanning, such as assuming a web application will run on port 80. Nessus provides both free and paid services, with certain features reserved for the paid version. While some functionalities are excluded from the free service to incentivize users to opt for the paid version, the free version remains adequate for our penetration testing requirements.

2.4.4 Metasploit

Metasploit is a framework designed for developing and automating the exploitation of vulnerabilities in computer systems, primarily used for penetration testing and vulnerability assessment. It stands as one of the most widely used operating frameworks in this field, offering robust support across all phases of a penetration test, from information gathering to post-exploitation activities. Metasploit exists in two main versions:

- **Metasploit Pro**: The commercial iteration that streamlines automation and task management, featuring a GUI.
- **Metasploit framework**: The open-source variant that operates from the command line interface (CLI).

The Metasploit framework encompasses a suite of tools enabling various tasks, including information gathering, analysis, exploitation, exploit development, post-exploitation activities, and more. While its primary application lies in penetration testing, it also proves valuable for vulnerability research and exploit development. Key components of the Metasploit framework include:

- **msfconsole**: The primary command-line interface.
- **Modules**: Versatile modules encompassing exploits, scanners, payloads, etc.
- **Tools**: Stand-alone utilities facilitating vulnerability scanning, assessment, or penetration testing, including tools like msfvenom, pattern_create, and pattern_offset.

2.4.5 Cobalt Strike

Cobalt Strike stands as a commercial adversary simulation software predominantly utilized by red teams and extensively during comprehensive penetration tests. However, it has also been illicitly acquired and deployed by a broad spectrum of malicious actors, ranging from ransomware operators to APTs focused on espionage. Understanding the myriad components and features of Cobalt Strike often necessitates substantial hands-on experience and study. At its core, Cobalt Strike functions as the command and control (C2) application, comprising two primary components: the team server and the client interface. These components are encapsulated within the same Java executable (JAR file), with the distinction lying solely in the arguments utilized by an operator during execution.

2.4.6 Burp suite

It is a web application security testing tool capable of scanning vulnerabilities, intercepting and modifying web traffic, and automating attacks.

2.4.7 Wireshark

Wireshark serves as an open-source network protocol analyzer, enabling real-time capture and analysis of network traffic. Whether scrutinizing local or remote networks, Wireshark grants comprehensive visibility into data packets traversing cables and airwaves. For both cybersecurity novices and seasoned network professionals, Wireshark offers numerous advantages:

- **Network issue identification**: Wireshark facilitates the examination of network traffic to pinpoint performance issues, outages, congestion, and configuration errors. It aids in the swift detection of bottlenecks, expediting issue resolution.
- **Threat analysis**: Utilizing Wireshark, users can dissect malicious traffic to uncover network attacks like DoS attacks, phishing attempts, and intrusion endeavors. This empowers proactive network security measures and fortification against potential threats.
- **Protocol familiarization**: Wireshark allows for the study of various network protocols such as TCP/IP, DNS, and HTTP. This fosters a deeper comprehension of network functionalities, enhancing the ability to diagnose and address network issues effectively.

2.4.8 Aircrack-ng

A suite of tools designed for testing Wi-Fi network security typically includes functionalities for detecting packets, capturing handshakes, and cracking passwords.

2.4.9 John the ripper

A popular password cracking tool that launches brute force attacks against password hash functions is Hashcat. Hashcat is an open-source password recovery tool that supports various algorithms and attack modes for cracking password hashes.

2.4.10 SQLmap

A tool commonly used to automate the process of exploiting SQL injection vulnerabilities in web applications is SQLmap. SQLmap is an open-source penetration testing tool that automates the detection and exploitation of SQL injection flaws in web applications. It helps security professionals assess the security of web applications by identifying and exploiting SQL injection vulnerabilities, potentially allowing unauthorized access to the underlying databases.

2.5 CONCLUSION

Offensive cybersecurity serves as a vital component in safeguarding digital assets, enabling organizations to proactively identify and rectify security weaknesses before they are exploited by malicious entities. This chapter underscores the significance of embracing advanced methodologies and tools to outpace the constantly evolving threat landscape. Through comprehensive insights into attacker techniques and corresponding defense strategies, cybersecurity practitioners are empowered with the requisite expertise and tactics to bolster their security posture. Addressing the complexities and ethical dimensions inherent in offensive cybersecurity underscores the need for ongoing innovation and education, ensuring resilient and preemptive defenses against both present and emerging cyber threats.

REFERENCES

[1] M. Ouaissa, and M. Ouaissa, "Cyber security issues for IoT based smart grid infrastructure," IOP Conference Series: Materials Science and Engineering, vol. 937, no. 1, 2020, p. 012001.
[2] Z. Zhou, and D. Qi, "Offensive corporate strategy and collaborative innovation," Finance Research Letters, vol. 58, 2023, p. 104414.
[3] C. Nobles, and I. Mcandrew, "The intersectionality of offensive cybersecurity and human factors: A position paper," Scientific Bulletin, vol. 28, no. 2, 2023, pp. 215–233.
[4] M. Jafari, M. Mohammadpour Omran, and E. Jahani, "Offensive, defensive, and generic advertising strategies in a dynamic oligopolistic market," Mathematical Problems in Engineering, vol. 2021, 2021, pp. 1–29.
[5] I. D. Aiyanyo, H. Samuel, and H. Lim, "A systematic review of defensive and offensive cybersecurity with machine learning," Applied Sciences, vol. 10, no. 17, 2020, p. 5811.
[6] D. Lakshmi, N. Nagpal, and S. Chandrasekaran, "A quantum-based approach for offensive security against cyber attacks in electrical infrastructure," Applied Soft Computing, vol. 136, 2023, p. 110071.

[7] S. Chng, H. Y. Lu, A. Kumar, and D. Yau, "Hacker types, motivations and strategies: A comprehensive framework," Computers in Human Behavior Reports, vol. 5, 2022, p. 100167.

[8] M. Alhamed, and M. H. Rahman, "A systematic literature review on penetration testing in networks: Future research directions," Applied Sciences, vol. 13, no. 12, 2023, p. 6986.

[9] D. Stiawan, M. Y. Idris, A. H. Abdullah, F. Aljaber, and R. Budiarto, "Cyber-attack penetration test and vulnerability analysis," International Journal of Online Engineering, vol. 13, no. 1, 2017, pp. 125–132.

[10] H. B. U. Haq, M. Z. Hassan, M. Z. Hussain, R. A. Khan, S. Nawaz, H. R. Khokhar, and M. Arshad, "The impacts of ethical hacking and its security mechanisms," Pakistan Journal of Engineering and Technology, vol. 5, no. 4, 2022, pp. 29–35.

[11] P. K. Gavel, R. Prasad, N. Rathore, and D. Yadav, "Ethical hacking and cyber security against cyber attacks," International Journal of Technology, vol. 10, no. 1, 2020, pp. 83–87.

[12] P. Chen, L. Desmet, and C. Huygens, "A study on advanced persistent threats," In Communications and Multimedia Security: 15th IFIP TC 6/TC 11 International Conference, CMS 2014, Aveiro, September 25–26, pp. 63–72. Berlin; Heidelberg: Springer, 2014.

[13] C. Gan, J. Lin, D. W. Huang, Q. Zhu, and L. Tian, "Advanced persistent threats and their defense methods in industrial Internet of things: A survey," Mathematics, vol. 11, no. 14, 2023, p. 3115.

[14] F. M. Al-Matarneh, "Advanced persistent threats and its role in network security vulnerabilities," International Journal of Advanced Research in Computer Science, vol. 11, no. 1, 2020, pp. 11–20.

[15] J. N. Goel, and B. M. Mehtre, "Vulnerability assessment & penetration testing as a cyber defence technology," Procedia Computer Science, vol. 57, 2015, pp. 710–715.

[16] T. J. Grant, "Tools and technologies for professional offensive cyber operations," International Journal of Cyber Warfare and Terrorism (IJCWT), vol. 3, no. 3, 2013, pp. 49–71.

Chapter 3

Defensive cybersecurity tools and technologies

3.1 INTRODUCTION

Defensive security employs traditional, tried-and-tested defense methods and measures to shield businesses from cyber threats. These approaches encompass security analysis, prevention measures, attack recognition, and response strategies. Often, software and network vulnerabilities stem from a lack of adherence to defensive security standards, which adept cybercriminals readily exploit. Hence, it is more crucial than ever to assess overall security posture and enhance the defensive capabilities of staff through comprehensive information security training [1].

Defensive security measures are oriented toward identifying perpetrators and, where possible, neutralizing or disrupting their operations. Reactive measures, such as software patching and remediation of system vulnerabilities, constitute a significant aspect of defensive activity. Defensive cybersecurity tactics include deploying firewalls, intrusion detection and prevention systems (IDS and IPS), antivirus software, encryption technologies, access controls, security policies, and employee training programs [2]. The overarching objective of defensive cybersecurity is to mitigate risks, safeguard critical information assets, uphold data CIA, and fortify IT infrastructures against cyber threats and attacks [3].

This chapter offers an overview of key measures and methodologies in defensive cybersecurity, including endpoint security solutions. The structure of the chapter is organized as follows. Section 3.2 provides insights into defensive strategies and underscores the importance of defense in depth. Sections 3.3 and 3.4 delve into defensive cybersecurity tools and advanced techniques utilized in emerging technologies. Section 3.5 elaborates on cloud security tools. Conclusions are summarized in Section 3.6.

3.2 UNDERSTANDING DEFENSIVE CYBERSECURITY

3.2.1 Overview of defensive strategies

Cyber defense entails the capability to thwart cyberattacks from infiltrating a network, computer system, or endpoint. It requires proactive measures to anticipate potential threats and respond to intrusions while minimizing their impact. Defensive strategies enable organizations to preemptively address emerging risks, ensuring preparedness during critical situations. Cyber defense empowers organizations to prevent cyberattacks through a myriad of cybersecurity solutions, techniques, and technologies. It comprises a blend of processes and practices aimed at safeguarding networks, data, and endpoints against unauthorized access or manipulation. This encompasses deploying and maintaining software and hardware infrastructure to deter hackers, as well as analyzing, identifying, and remedying system vulnerabilities. Additionally, real-time solutions are implemented to counter zero-day attacks. Effective cyber defense also encompasses the ability to recover from successful cyberattacks [4].

3.2.2 Importance of defense in depth

Defense in depth, a cybersecurity strategy, employs a variety of security products and practices to safeguard an organization's network, web properties, and resources. Sometimes synonymous with layered security, it relies on multiple levels of control—physical, technical, and administrative—to thwart attackers from breaching a protected network or on-premises resource. The core tenet of this strategy acknowledges that a single security product cannot fully shield a network against all potential attacks. However, through the implementation of diverse security products and practices, organizations can enhance their ability to detect and prevent attacks, effectively mitigating a broad range of threats. This approach is particularly vital as organizations expand their networks, systems, and user base [5].

3.3 COMMON DEFENSIVE CYBERSECURITY TOOLS

3.3.1 Firewall technologies

A firewall is a combination of software and hardware components that determine whether traffic is permitted to enter or leave a local network or computer. The primary function of a firewall is to block certain data transfer requests. It makes these decisions based on a set of predefined rules applied to each packet; packet filtering can occur at multiple layers. This monitoring of all network traffic enables the isolation, to some extent, of potential malicious traffic [6].

3.3.1.1 Operating modes

There are various types of firewalls, including:

By operating mode:

Firewalls utilize three basic methods or services to protect the network and can be classified based on the services used. The three types are as follows:

- **Packet filtering:** This method examines the packet header, checks the IP address, port, or both, and grants or denies access without making any changes. It includes traditional firewalls and stateful firewalls.
- **Circuit proxy:** The main distinction between circuit proxy and packet filtering firewall is that the former acts as the recipient to which all communicators should address their packets. The circuit proxy replaces the original address with its own address before forwarding packets to the desired destination.
- **Application proxy:** This method is more complex in operation compared to the previous two. It involves the application protocol and the data, and based on this information, it makes decisions.

By installation:

- **Per-host firewall:** It controls incoming and outgoing traffic from a single computer.
- **Network firewall:** It controls incoming and outgoing traffic from a network. It can be installed on a router (as software) or as a dedicated device (e.g., CISCO ASA).

As part of cybersecurity monitoring, malicious traffic detected by the firewall can be collected and analyzed from log files.

3.3.1.2 Next-generation firewall

For many businesses, the primary line of defense for their network is a next-generation firewall (NGFW). Similar to a traditional firewall, an NGFW inspects all incoming and outgoing network traffic and establishes a barrier between internal and external networks based on trust principles, rules, and other administrative parameters. Additionally, it integrates additional features such as application recognition and control, IPS, and cybersecurity monitoring services. While a NGFW is a crucial component of the overall network security strategy, it does not provide complete protection on its own and should be complemented with other security tools and technologies. It is also worth noting that traditional firewalls are now considered obsolete due to their inability to effectively block advanced attacks, particularly in cloud environments. Consequently, businesses are encouraged to upgrade to an NGFW solution [7].

3.3.1.3 Web application firewall

WAF is a security tool engineered to safeguard businesses at the application level. It achieves this by filtering, monitoring, and analyzing Hypertext Transfer Protocol (HTTP) and Hypertext Transfer Protocol Secure (HTTPS) traffic between web applications and the Internet.

3.3.2 Intrusion detection systems

An IDS can be a combination of software and hardware capable of analyzing network traffic to detect and identify malicious activity. The objective of the IDS is to alert but not to act; the information obtained by the IDS regarding detected activity is typically more specific and detailed than that obtained by a firewall. Most IDSs aim to accomplish their tasks in real time. However, there are also IDSs that do not operate in real time, either due to the nature of the analysis they perform or because they are intended for forensic analysis [8]. The operation of the IDS is based on the detection of malicious traffic using two techniques:

- **The signature-based approach:** This relies on an attack signature database consisting of a set of definitions of known threat models with specific characteristics.
- **The behavioral approach:** Also known as anomaly detection, this approach has the advantage of being able to discover attacks that have not yet been recorded. They generally operate in two phases: a learning phase, which defines certain criteria for the normal operation of the system or network, and a detection phase. During the detection phase, if detected network traffic does not correspond to the defined criteria, the IDS can identify it as malicious traffic.

IDS has two main issues: false positives and false negatives.

- **False positives:** These are events reported as alerts but are not actually indicative of malicious traffic.
- **False negatives:** These are malicious events occurring on the network but not detected by the IDS.

False negatives may pose a greater risk, as it is more preferable to detect nonexistent threats than to miss actual malicious activity. False positives can also be counterproductive, particularly in cybersecurity monitoring and the analysis of malicious traffic for threat intelligence purposes.

IDS can be categorized based on several criteria, such as location, monitoring approaches, and analysis techniques (Figure 3.1).

The most common way to classify IDS is by grouping them according to location:

- **Host-based IDS (HIDS):** Host-based intrusion detection systems, or HIDS (Host IDS), analyze network traffic entering and exiting a specific device, changes in the file system, and system activity in general (Figure 3.2).

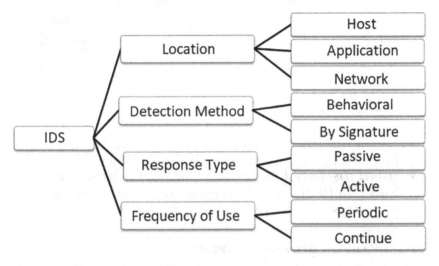

Figure 3.1 Characteristics of IDSs

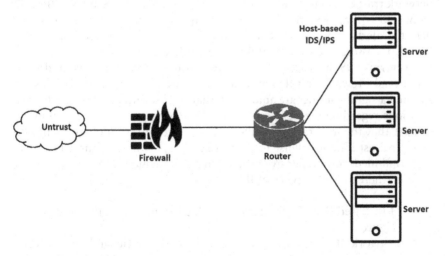

Figure 3.2 Host-based IDS/IPS

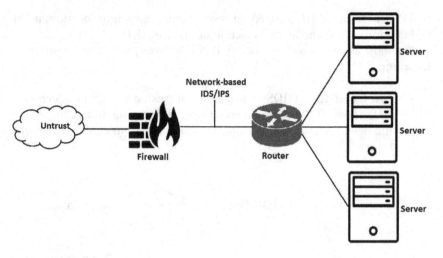

Figure 3.3 Network IDS/IPS

- **Network IDS (NIDS):** NIDS analyzes network traffic and receives data from all computers connected to the network (Figure 3.3).
- **Hybrid IDS:** Hybrid IDSs utilize a distributed architecture that combines both HIDS and NIDS functionalities. Information is sent to a single IDS server. Such systems can be beneficial in large networks.

3.3.3 Intrusion prevention systems

IPS, like IDS, is a combination of software and hardware designed to analyze network traffic to detect and identify malicious activity. The main difference from IDS is that IPS are active devices capable of taking action based on detected alerts, thereby preventing attacks in real time, which implies that IPS also possess firewall capabilities [9]. While some may argue that IPS outperforms IDS due to the increasingly serious network security landscape, traditional firewalls and IDS may fall short of meeting user needs. This has sparked a significant debate among international security and research organizations regarding the obsolescence of IDS. However, contrasting opinions suggest that the integration of IPS, IDS, and firewall technologies will provide a robust line of defense to protect systems. With these three technologies combined, comprehensive protection can be achieved for any system. In general, there are three types of IPS:

- **Host-based IPS (HIPS):** It monitors local computer traffic and activity (Figure 3.2).
- **Network IPS (NIPS):** It analyzes network traffic and must receive data from all computers connected to the network. It allows for

the monitoring of traffic from multiple computers on the network (Figure 3.3).

3.3.4 Antivirus software

Antivirus software is essential for protecting against viruses and malware. However, many variants often rely on signature-based detection. While these solutions provide robust protection against known malware, signature-based products can be exploited by savvy cybercriminals. Therefore, it is prudent to utilize antivirus solutions that incorporate heuristic functions capable of analyzing and detecting suspicious patterns and activities. NGAV is a network security tool that integrates AI, behavior detection, ML algorithms, and exploit mitigation to proactively anticipate and prevent all types of threats, both known and unknown. NGAVs are typically cloud-based, enabling swift and efficient deployment while alleviating the burden associated with software installation and maintenance, infrastructure management, and signature database upkeep for IT or information security teams.

3.3.5 Vulnerability assessment tools

A protocol analyzer is a piece of computer hardware or software used to capture and record packets flowing over a network for analysis, storage, and presentation in a user-friendly format. Protocol analyzers, also known as network analyzers or packet analyzers, are essential tools for diagnosing network problems and detecting intrusion attempts and malicious traffic. They offer a comprehensive set of primitives for filtering and selecting traffic based on various header fields and payload values. Due to their ability to decode packets of major IP protocols such as TCP, UDP, ICMP, and some higher-level protocols like DNS, they are considered tools for deep analysis of network traffic. However, it is important to note that these tools can also be used for malicious purposes, such as capturing traffic to obtain private information. Using them effectively requires a deep understanding of network protocols and datagram analysis—the techniques and theory needed to interpret content accurately. The primary objective of packet analyzers is to provide information about network traffic that can be used to determine whether it is malicious and to gather threat intelligence [10].

Many IDS, IPS, or firewalls utilize this type of tool as an engine to capture network traffic at a lower level, allowing real-time analysis. However, the key difference lies in the fact that they generally only store network packets for which certain alerts were detected. Some of the most well-known tools based on the libpcap library include tcpdump, Windump, WireShark, and TShark.

3.4 ADVANCED DEFENSIVE TECHNIQUES AND TECHNOLOGIES

3.4.1 Incident detection and response

3.4.1.1 Endpoint detection and response

EDR is a solution crafted to identify and probe cyber threats on endpoints, including PCs, laptops, or servers. Unlike traditional antivirus software, EDR does not solely rely on scanning files for virus signatures but also scrutinizes endpoint behavior. Upon detecting suspicious behavior, the tool notifies the IT security team and proposes corrective actions [11]. Additionally, EDR tools can automate mitigation responses, such as endpoint isolation. Key features of EDR include:

- Terminal monitoring and event recording
- Data research, investigation, and threat hunting
- Detection of suspicious activities
- Provision of suggested corrective measures
- Automated response for mitigation measures.

3.4.1.2 Extended detection and response

Extended detection and response (XDR) signifies the advancement of EDR solutions, broadening the horizon of detection beyond endpoints. It encompasses detection, analysis, and response functionalities across various data sources. By collecting data and scrutinizing the behavior of all IT layers and applications, XDR extends its coverage beyond endpoints to encompass network components and cloud services. This comprehensive approach offers a holistic perspective on IT security and potential cyber threats, thereby simplifying investigation and response endeavors. Key features of XDR include:

- Monitoring data sources across different domains
- Data research, investigation, and threat hunting across various domains
- Analysis of threat-oriented events
- Detection of suspicious activities
- Provision of suggested corrective measures
- Enhanced automated mitigation response capabilities

3.4.1.3 Security information and event management

Security information and event management (SIEM) is a solution empowering organizations to consolidate, correlate, and analyze computer network data for security issue detection. Key components of SIEM encompass log management and centralization, security event detection, and reporting and search functionalities. It facilitates analysts in examining log and event data, as well as in monitoring and documenting security information for compliance and auditing objectives. SIEM solutions empower IT security teams to:

- Collect and correlate log data
- Utilize data to identify, classify, and analyze incidents and events
- Consolidate multi-domain data into a central platform
- Generate alerts and reports
- Support incident response efforts
- Store logging data for compliance and auditing purposes

3.4.1.4 Security orchestration, automation, and response

SOAR serves as a solution augmenting and enriching SIEM platforms. It aims to enhance event data, simplify the identification of critical incidents, and automate response actions triggered by specific events or triggers. The goal is to escalate threats solely when human intervention is deemed essential. SOAR solutions empower IT security teams to:

- Gather information about security threats from various sources and centralize it
- Automate responses to security threats
- Minimize the need for human intervention

3.4.1.5 Managed detection and response

MDR is a service that encompasses security monitoring, analysis, and threat response components. Although software is essential, the key determinant for the success of an MDR service lies in the presence of highly skilled analysts. The expertise of these analysts often marks the difference between success and failure. The MDR service comprises:

- IT security analysts
- The process
- IT security tools
- Continuous security monitoring
- Threat hunting
- Prioritization of threats and alerts
- Security analysis
- Security response measures

3.4.1.6 Security Operations Center

Security Operations Center (SOC) functions as a centralized command center engineered to protect the IT infrastructure of organizations. It assumes responsibility for monitoring vital systems, assessing and mitigating threats, and coordinating incident response efforts. SOC analysts commonly collaborate with cybersecurity specialists from diverse domains, utilizing specialized tools in synchronized processes. A traditional SOC comprises:

- A central control center
- IT security analysts
- Processes
- IT security tools
- Various IT security services

3.4.2 Network segmentation

Network segmentation is simply the division of a computer network into smaller logical or physical components. Two devices located on the same network can communicate without an intermediary. However, for devices located on different segments to exchange data, traffic must pass through an external demarcation point. This policy aids in traffic analysis or the application of security policies, thereby enhancing overall security. Network segmentation stands as one of the most effective strategies against data leaks, ransomware infections, and other cybersecurity threats. There are numerous strategies for effectively segmenting a network, but Virtual Local Area Networks (VLANs) and subnetting are among the most popular [12].

3.4.2.1 Microsegmentation

Traditionally, businesses use network segmentation to segregate different types of traffic and isolate sensitive resources. By defining network segments based on parameters such as device type or geography, simple segmentation can restrict exposure to threats. However, this approach has its limitations. Once an attacker breaches the security perimeter and infiltrates a segment, they can move laterally without obstruction. This is where microsegmentation comes into play. It subdivides the network into smaller segments, or microsegments, each with its own set of security policies, thereby limiting an attacker's lateral movement even after an initial intrusion. Microsegmentation operates on the principle of "zero trust," assuming that an attacker may already be within the network. As a result, each microsegment is treated as an independent network with its own security rules.

3.4.2.2 Zero trust architecture

Zero trust is a security framework that mandates all users, whether internal or external to the company network, to undergo authentication, authorization, and continuous validation of their configuration and security level before being granted or retaining access to data and applications. It is a network security philosophy asserting that no individual inside or outside the network should be inherently trusted without careful verification of their identity. Zero trust operates under the assumption that threats both outside and inside the network are omnipresent. It also assumes that every attempt to access the network or application poses a potential threat. These assumptions guide network administrators to design stringent and robust security measures [13]. Implementing zero trust necessitates rigorous verification of the identity of each individual or device attempting to access the network or application. This verification process applies irrespective of whether the device or user is already within the network perimeter. Events such as changes in devices used, location, login frequency, or the number of failed login attempts can trigger identity verification for users or devices.

Zero trust architecture is a comprehensive framework promising effective protection of an organization's most valuable assets. It operates under the premise that every connection and endpoint is a potential threat. The framework guards against these threats, whether they originate externally or internally, even for internal connections.

3.4.3 Multifactor authentication

Authentication is simply the process of verifying your identity to access networks, accounts, or systems. However, authenticating an account solely with a simple password has become less secure as cybercriminals become increasingly adept at accessing accounts through password attacks. Most people do not use strong, unique passwords for each of their accounts, putting them at greater risk of having their accounts compromised [14].

Single sign-on (SSO) is a method that allows a user to access several computer applications by completing only one authentication process. SSO is an authentication solution that enables users to sign in to multiple applications and websites with a single login. SSO provides convenience because once users' identities are validated, they can access any password-protected resources without having to log in multiple times.

Two-factor authentication (2FA) is a form of authentication that requires two authentication factors. The first factor is your username and password, while the second is another method of your choice [15].

MFA is a form of authentication that requires one or more additional authentication factors. Similar to 2FA, the first factor is your username and password, and the others can be chosen according to your preference. MFA serves as a central mechanism that enhances the security of user accounts and access on a system. It is an authentication method that helps prevent various malicious attacks and exploits aimed at compromising data, such as brute force attacks, session hijacking, and elevation of privileges. Several types of factors can be used for MFA:

- Knowledge factors: password, PIN, etc.
- Physical factors: smartphone, security token, USB key, etc.
- Biological factors: fingerprint, facial or voice recognition, etc.
- Location factors: network connection, geographical position, etc.

3.4.4 Data loss prevention

Data loss prevention (DLP) is a component of an overall enterprise security strategy that encompasses the detection and prevention of data loss, leaks, or misuse through compromise, exfiltration, and unauthorized use. Some DLP solutions also include alerting, encryption enablement, and data isolation capabilities in the event a compromise or other security incident is detected.

3.4.5 Privileged access management and identity and access management

Privileged access management (PAM) is the process of defining and controlling privileged users and administrator accounts to limit identity-driven malware attacks and prevent unauthorized access to the network or related resources. PAM stands as one of the most effective preventative processes and systems available to organizations seeking to reduce the risks posed by their employees, partners, suppliers, systems, and third parties. PAM defines which employees, partners, vendors, and even applications have access to your specific accounts and data, providing you with control and flexibility. Implementing PAM is achieved through a combination of software, defined processes, and enforcement that restrict access to your most critical data and resources to only those individuals and applications with privileged access. It also serves as a means to monitor users with high-level access and ensure the safety of your assets and data.

Identity and access management (IAM) refers to a set of policies and technologies enabling IT managers to control everyday user access to specific applications and information within the enterprise. With the rise in cyberattacks and increasing regulatory pressure on businesses to control access to corporate information, IAM is increasingly recognized as an essential framework for protecting systems and data.

PAM constitutes a subset of IAM that exclusively focuses on safeguarding privileged accounts, accounts granted to a select number of users who require access to backend systems, databases, and other locations where highly sensitive information is stored. While the IAM solution securely authorizes any user needing access to a system, the PAM solution restricts access rights to the absolute minimum number of users necessary to carry out authorized business activities.

3.5 CLOUD SECURITY TOOLS

3.5.1 Cloud access security brokers

Cloud access security broker (CASB) is an on-premises or cloud-based security policy enforcement point situated between users and cloud service providers. It consolidates and applies enterprise security policies when users access resources in the cloud. Think of the CASB as the sheriff enforcing laws set by cloud service administrators. Organizations increasingly rely on CASBs to manage cloud service risks, enforce security policies, and comply with applicable regulations, even when the affected cloud services are beyond their perimeter and direct control [16]. A CASB serves as an intermediary between users and cloud computing platforms, safeguarding data in the cloud while addressing authorization and visibility concerns for businesses using cloud computing services. The CASB process unfolds in three stages:

* Discovery: CASB scans and identifies resources provisioned on the enterprise's cloud infrastructure.
* Classification: Once the CASB has discovered all cloud resources, each component is assigned a risk value, enabling the classification and rating of applications and data based on their significance.
* Remediation: With data classified, the organization can utilize the classification designations to enforce appropriate access controls and take necessary action in response to unauthorized requests.

3.5.2 Cloud security posture management

Cloud security posture management (CSPM) is a cybersecurity technology that automates and consolidates the identification and resolution of configuration issues and security risks across hybrid and multicloud environments and services, including Infrastructure as a Service (IaaS), Platform as a Service (PaaS), and Software as a Service (SaaS).

The CSPM approach monitors cloud resources to alert administrators of misconfigurations and potential vulnerabilities that could be exploited by attackers. While cloud platforms are generally secure, administrators who underestimate threats and neglect proper configurations often contribute to significant cloud data breaches. CSPM entails the use of policies and soft-ware to ensure that cloud resources are audited, organized, properly config-ured, maintained, secure, and compliant with industry standards.

3.5.3 IAM in the cloud

IAM in the cloud refers to the administration of identities and access rights to IT resources within a cloud computing environment. In an IAM system, each user or entity is assigned unique identifiers that authenticate them when accessing cloud services. In addition to authentication, IAM also governs the permissions and privileges granted to each user or entity, determining their allowed actions once connected to the cloud. Key features of cloud IAM include:

- **Authentication:** This involves verification of the identity of a user or entity, often achieved through identifiers such as usernames and pass-words, API keys, digital certificates, or MFA methods.
- **Authorization:** This is an assignment of specific access rights to users or entities once authenticated. This may entail access to specific resources, the ability to read, write, modify, or delete data, and other privileges.
- **Privilege management:** Control over the privileges granted to each user or entity, including the ability to adjust these privileges based on the user's needs and roles.
- **Identity management:** Creation, management, and deletion of user accounts and entities, as well as the management of associated infor-mation such as personal data, roles, and attributes.

Cloud IAM is vital for ensuring the security and compliance of data and resources in a distributed IT environment, enabling organizations to cen-trally oversee and manage access to cloud services.

3.6 CONCLUSION

Defensive cybersecurity plays a critical role in safeguarding digital assets against cyber threats and attacks. This chapter delved into the fundamentals of defensive cybersecurity, emphasizing the significance of tools and tech-nologies for identifying, preventing, detecting, and responding to security incidents. By examining a diverse array of defense mechanisms in detail, we underscored their indispensable role in shielding networks, systems, and data from malicious activities. Nevertheless, it is essential to acknowledge that cybersecurity remains an ongoing challenge, necessitating continual vigilance and adaptation to evolving cyber threats. Through investments in cutting-edge technologies, reinforcement of security practices, and promotion of user awareness, organizations can fortify their defensive posture and mitigate the risks associated with cyberattacks.

REFERENCES

[1] O. C. Obi, O. V. Akagha, S. O. Dawodu, A. C. Anyanwu, S. Onwusinkwue, and I. A. I. Ahmad, "Comprehensive review on cybersecurity: Modern threats and advanced defense strategies," Computer Science & IT Research Journal, vol. 5, no. 2, 2024, pp. 293–310.

[2] M. Ouaissa, and M. Ouaissa, "Cyber security issues for IoT based smart grid infrastructure," IOP Conference Series: Materials Science and Engineering, vol. 937, no. 1, 2020, p. 012001.

[3] Y. Zheng, Z. Li, X. Xu, and Q. Zhao, "Dynamic defenses in cyber security: Techniques, methods and challenges," Digital Communications and Networks, vol. 8, no. 4, 2022, pp. 422–435.

[4] M. Sulaiman, M. Waseem, A. N. Ali, G. Laouini, and F. S. Alshammari, "Defense strategies for epidemic cyber security threats: Modeling and analysis by using a machine learning approach," IEEE Access, vol. 12, 2024, pp. 4958–4984.

[5] M. N. Dazahra, F. Elmariami, A. Belfqih, and J. Boukherouaa, "A defense-in-depth cybersecurity for smart substations," International Journal of Electrical and Computer Engineering (IJECE), vol. 8, no. 6, 2018, pp. 4423–4431.

[6] P. Wang, "Research on firewall technology and its application in computer network security strategy," Frontiers in Computing and Intelligent Systems, vol. 2, no. 2, 2022, pp. 42–46.

[7] X. He, "Research on computer network security based on firewall technology," Journal of Physics: Conference Series, vol. 1744, no. 4, 2021, p. 042037.

[8] A. Khraisat, I. Gondal, P. Vamplew, and J. Kamruzzaman, "Survey of intrusion detection systems: Techniques, datasets and challenges," Cybersecurity, vol. 2, no. 1, 2019, pp. 1–22.

[9] S. H. Abbas, W. A. K. Naser, and A. A. Kadhim, "Subject review: Intrusion Detection System (IDS) and Intrusion Prevention System (IPS)," Global Journal of Engineering and Technology Advances, vol. 14, no. 2, 2023, pp. 155–158.

[10] D. Du, M. Zhu, X. Li, M. Fei, S. Bu, L. Wu, and K. Li, "A review on cybersecurity analysis, attack detection, and attack defense methods in cyber-physical power systems," Journal of Modern Power Systems and Clean Energy, vol. 11, no. 3, 2022, pp. 727–743.

[11] M. Plachkinova, and K. Knapp, "Least privilege across people, process, and technology: Endpoint security framework," Journal of Computer Information Systems, vol. 63, no. 5, 2023, pp. 1153–1165.

[12] D. Galinec, D. Možnik, and B. Guberina, "Cybersecurity and cyber defence: National level strategic approach," Automatika: časopis za automatiku, mjerenje, elektroniku, računarstvo i komunikacije, vol. 58, no. 3, 2017, pp. 273–286.

[13] H. Kang, G. Liu, Q. Wang, L. Meng, and J. Liu, "Theory and application of zero trust security: A brief survey," Entropy, vol. 25, no. 12, 2023, p. 1595.
[14] J. Williamson, and K. Curran, "The role of multi-factor authentication for modern day security," Semiconductor Science and Information Devices, vol. 3, no. 1, 2021, pp. 16–23.
[15] M. Ouaissa, and M. Ouaissa, "An improved privacy authentication protocol for 5G mobile networks," In 2020 International Conference on Advances in Computing, Communication & Materials (ICACCM), pp. 136–143. New York: IEEE, 2020.
[16] M. Chauhan, and S. Shiaeles, "An analysis of cloud security frameworks, problems and proposed solutions," Network, vol. 3, no. 3, 2023, pp. 422–450.

Chapter 4

Threat modeling and risk management

4.1 INTRODUCTION

Threat modeling is an effective approach to securing systems, applications, networks, and services. It employs engineering techniques to identify threats and offer recommendations for reducing risks, thus achieving security objectives earlier in the development life cycle. Risk management is integral to an organization's security strategy [1]. By proactively identifying, assessing, prioritizing, and mitigating risks, organizations safeguard their assets, ensure business continuity, and minimize potential losses. Effective risk management necessitates a structured and ongoing approach, involving regular assessments and adjustments based on the evolving threat landscape and organizational changes [2].

The integration of threat modeling and risk management is explored, advocating for a holistic approach to comprehensive security [3]. Case studies demonstrate the practical application of these concepts, while best practices underscore the importance of cultivating a security-centric culture, continuously reassessing threats and risks, and fostering interdepartmental collaboration [4].

This chapter elucidates the threat modeling methodology and its primary tools, alongside discussions on the principles of security policy and risk management. The structure of this chapter is as follows. Section 4.2 provides an overview of threat modeling, followed by Section 4.3 presenting the tools and techniques of threat modeling. Section 4.4 delves into IS security policy, while Section 4.5 discusses the risk management process. Conclusions are drawn in Section 4.6.

4.2 UNDERSTANDING THREAT MODELING

Threat modeling is an effective method for securing systems, applications, networks, and services. It involves identifying potential threats and providing recommendations to reduce risks and attain security objectives earlier

DOI: 10.1201/9781003509080-4

in the development life cycle [5]. A key aspect of threat modeling is the utilization of a data flow diagram, which visually illustrates how the system functions. Subsequently, a framework is applied to facilitate the identification and resolution of security issues. Systems released without prior threat modeling expose both customers and organizations to significant risks [6]. Threat modeling is a technique accessible to anyone familiar with their system's operation, possessing a basic understanding of information security. The technique is segmented into four distinct phases, each comprising crucial steps enabling the creation of a data flow diagram and its subsequent analysis for potential threats (Figure 4.1). Table 4.1 provides a description of each phase [7].

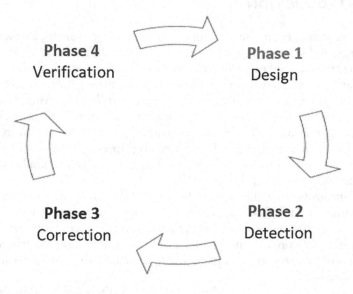

Figure 4.1 Threat modeling phases

Table 4.1 Description of the threat modeling phases

Phase	Title	Description
1	Design	Capture all your system requirements and create a data flow diagram.
2	Detection	Apply a threat modeling framework to the data flow diagram and find potential security issues.
3	Correction	Decide how to approach each issue with the appropriate combination of security controls.
4	Verification	Verify that requirements are met, issues are detected, and security controls are implemented.

4.3 TOOLS AND TECHNIQUES FOR THREAT MODELING

4.3.1 Microsoft threat modeling tool

The threat modeling tool is a vital component of the Microsoft Security Development Lifecycle (SDL). It empowers software architects to pinpoint and rectify potential security issues early in the development process, when they are relatively straightforward and cost-effective to address. Consequently, it substantially diminishes the overall development expenditure. Furthermore, we crafted this tool with non-security experts in mind, simplifying threat modeling for all developers by furnishing expert guidance on the creation and analysis of threat models [8]. This tool enables anyone to:

- Communicate about the security design of their systems.
- Analyze these designs for potential security issues using a proven methodology.
- Propose and manage corrective measures for security issues.

Typically, Microsoft employs STRIDE, an acronym representing six major threat categories that offer an extensive, though not exhaustive, list of threats [9]. To assist in formulating specific questions, Microsoft utilizes the STRIDE model, which categorizes various types of threats and streamlines overall security discussions. The threats encompass spoofing, tampering, repudiation, information disclosure, DoS, and elevation of privilege [10].

- **Spoofing:** It involves the illicit acquisition and use of another user's authentication credentials, such as usernames and passwords.
- **Tampering:** It entails the malicious alteration of data. Examples include unauthorized modifications to persistent data, such as that housed in a database, and manipulation of data traversing between two computers over an open network, such as the Internet.
- **Repudiation:** It concerns users disavowing actions without the ability for other parties to substantiate otherwise. For instance, a user executes an illicit operation within a system lacking the capability to track prohibited actions. Non-repudiation refers to a system's capacity to counter repudiation threats. For example, a user making a purchase may be required to provide a signature upon receiving the item. The supplier can then employ the signed acknowledgment of receipt as evidence of the item's delivery to the user.
- **Information disclosure:** It encompasses the exposure of information to unauthorized individuals. It also includes instances where users can access files they are not authorized to view or intruders intercepting data in transit between two computers.

- **Denial of service:** DoS attacks obstruct legitimate users from accessing services, such as rendering a web server temporarily unavailable or unusable. Protecting against specific types of DoS threats is imperative to enhance system reliability and availability.
- **Elevation of privilege:** It occurs when an unprivileged user attains privileged access, thereby gaining sufficient control to compromise or dismantle the entire system. Elevation of privilege threats encompass scenarios where an attacker bypasses all system defenses and integrates into the trust system itself, presenting a highly perilous situation.

4.3.2 DREAD

This is another Microsoft methodology used for the risk assessment of identified threats. DREAD stands for damage potential, reproducibility, exploitability, affected users, and discoverability [11]. Each of these factors is evaluated, and the result is utilized to prioritize the identified threats.

- **Damage potential:** This criterion evaluates the potential damage that could occur if the threat is exploited. It considers the impact on CIA of data or system resources.
- **Reproducibility:** Reproducibility assesses the ease with which the threat can be replicated or exploited by an attacker. Threats that are easily reproducible are considered more severe.
- **Exploitability:** Exploitability measures the ease with which an attacker can exploit the vulnerability associated with the threat. Threats that are easy to exploit are considered more severe.
- **Affected users:** This criterion examines the number of users or systems that would be impacted if the threats were successfully exploited. Threats that affect a larger number of users are considered more severe.
- **Discoverability:** Discoverability assesses how easily the threat can be discovered or detected by an attacker. Threats that are difficult to detect are considered more severe.

DREAD is typically used during the design and development phases of a system or application to identify potential security vulnerabilities and prioritize them based on their severity. Each criterion is assigned a score, often on a scale from 0 to 10, with higher scores indicating greater severity. By evaluating threats using the DREAD model, organizations can focus their resources on addressing the most critical security risks and implementing appropriate countermeasures to mitigate them.

4.3.3 OWASP Threat Dragon

An open source project from OWASP, Threat Dragon is both a web and desktop application that includes system diagramming as well as a rules engine to automatically generate threats/mitigations. Threat modeling is a process used to identify and prioritize potential security threats and vulnerabilities in software applications. OWASP Threat Dragon provides a graphical interface for creating and visualizing threat models, making it easier for developers and security professionals to analyze and address security risks in their applications.

4.4 IS SECURITY POLICY

To deal with security attacks and protect the IS, any organization will need to carefully develop a security strategy, often called IS security policy. This policy translates into the development of a security framework for an organization [12]. It essentially includes the security objectives and rules to be applied as well as the actions to be carried out in order to provide an acceptable level of security. A policy addresses the security of all activities and sensitive information of an organization [13]. The main objectives of an IS security policy are as follows:

- Define the security objectives for an organization and develop the security rules to be put in place.
- Define a uniform approach, guaranteeing a high degree of security.
- Define responsibilities for IS security.

To develop an IS security policy offering the objectives described above, you must follow a well-organized and planned approach [14]. As illustrated in Figure 4.2, a policy approach, following best security practices, is organized in four phases:

Phase 0: Prerequisite

Phase 0 is a preliminary phase which must be carried out to determine all the elements necessary for the development of the PSSI.

Phase 1: Development of strategic elements

Phase 1 is the first phase of developing an IS security policy. During this phase, the information security manager, with the steering committee, conduct an information security risk analysis. An information security risk analysis includes several steps. The number, name, and execution process of these

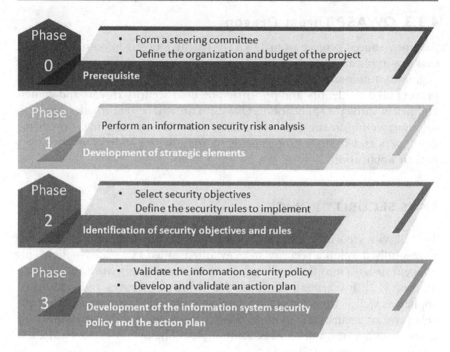

Figure 4.2 The phases of developing an IS security policy

steps differ depending on the standard or risk management method used. In fact, risk analysis is included in the risk management process.

Phase 2: Identification of security objectives and rules

After carrying out the information security risk analysis, the steering committee moves on to carrying out phase 2.

Phase 3: Development of an IS security policy and the action plan

Phase 3 is the last phase of developing an IS security policy.

4.5 RISK MANAGEMENT PROCESS

4.5.1 Concept general

Risk is defined as the potential for loss or damage when a threat exploits a vulnerability in an organization's information assets, including information technology infrastructure, applications, and data. It is a broad term that covers any type of risk, whether it is cybersecurity risk, power outage, disaster, human error, software/hardware failure, etc.; in short, anything that can disrupt a business and relies in one way or another on information technology. Risk management is the process of analyzing a threat to an organization's information technology infrastructure by assessing the level of risk it is willing to accept. This is what the industry calls "risk appetite." If the company cannot assume a specific risk, then it must determine whether the risk can be minimized and how to do so. Risk management does not always mean reducing risk to zero, but minimizing risk when the impact is significant [15].

4.5.1.1 Threat and vulnerability relationship

Risk is a fundamental concept in cybersecurity, often calculated using the following formula:

$$A + T + V = \textbf{Risk}$$

In this equation, A represents the asset, M denotes the threat, and V signifies the vulnerability.

- **Asset:** An asset pertains to sensitive data or anything that grants access to such data. It holds value, such as private information, a device, or a component within a system.
- **Threat:** The threat encompasses entities like malicious hackers, criminals, or insiders who aim to steal information. Additionally, threats can manifest as accidents, technical failures, or user errors that jeopardize data.
- **Vulnerability:** A vulnerability is a weakness capable of destroying, damaging, or endangering data. In software, vulnerabilities typically arise from flaws in a program's code (bugs) or how the program exposes or grants access to data.

The ISO 27000 family of standards pertaining to information security introduces the concept of impact to the risk definition. Evaluating impact involves prioritizing risks based on severity. For instance, a risk with high probability but low impact holds less significance and falls lower on the priority list compared to risks with lower probability but extremely high impact. By incorporating impact into the definition, the revised equation becomes:

$$V \times T \times I = \textbf{Risk}$$

4.5.1.2 Relationship probability and impact

Every risk event, whether it is a risk or an opportunity, possesses two key attributes: its likelihood of occurrence and the impact it would entail if it materialized. Even on the most straightforward projects, risk events should be evaluated for their probability and impact using a scale, such as high, medium, and low. As the complexity of the project grows, so should the sophistication of the assessment. For higher complexity projects and programs, a comprehensive risk event assessment typically employs a five-point scale, accompanied by guidelines and numerical values for each point on the scale.

4.5.2 EBIOS risk manager and ISO 27005

Risk management is a process aimed at identifying, assessing, and prioritizing threats and risks impacting an organization and its IS [16]. Its goal is to select appropriate security measures and action plans while proposing adjustments for existing security solutions. According to the ISO, risk management comprises a series of activities designed to guide an organization in addressing potential risks. The primary objectives of an IS risk management approach are as follows:

- Enhancing the security of the organization and its IS.
- Justifying the budget required to secure an IS.
- Demonstrating the credibility of the IS through conducted analyses.

IS risk management serves as a crucial tool for effective IS security policy.

4.5.2.1 Risk management process

Generally, a risk management process is iterative and typically comprises five overarching steps (Figure 4.3):

- Identification of the organization's scope and assets.
- Establishment of security objectives.
- Risk analysis, the core of the risk management process, involves:
  - Identifying vulnerabilities and threats associated with each asset.
  - Assessing the impact of risks associated with each asset.
  - Prioritizing risks by assessing the level of impact for each.
- Definition of security requirements, specifying the security risks to be addressed.
- Selection and implementation of security measures based on the outcomes of the preceding steps.

The process outlined above is widely accepted by the majority of risk management methods and standards. However, terminology may vary among different standards or methods. Additionally, some standards/methods embrace the principle of continuous improvement, while others do not.

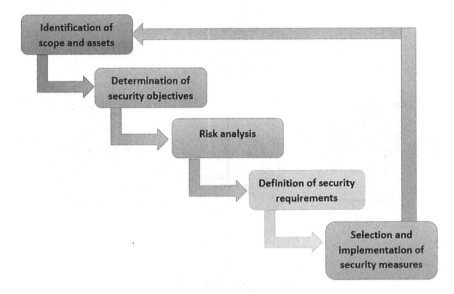

Figure 4.3 Phases of the risk management process

4.5.2.2 EBIOS method

The EBIOS method is a formal risk management method which is organized into five modules (Figure 4.4). EBIOS describes an iterative approach which is updated continuously. In fact, each module can be reviewed several times to improve its content.

- The first module of the EBIOS approach is Context Study. This module serves to formalize the study framework and determine the elements necessary for conducting the risk management process.
- The second module, Study of Feared Events, focuses on examining all feared events by assessing the severity level of each. Feared events are undesirable occurrences not in line with safety requirements. This module consists of a single activity, which is the assessment of feared events.
- The third module, Study of Threat Scenarios, involves studying all threat scenarios by evaluating the likelihood of each scenario. This module comprises a single activity: assessing threat scenarios.
- The fourth module, Risk Study, is dedicated to identifying potential risk scenarios within the study area by establishing correlations between feared events and threat scenarios. Additionally, risk assessment (prioritization) occurs in this module to facilitate the selection of appropriate security measures.

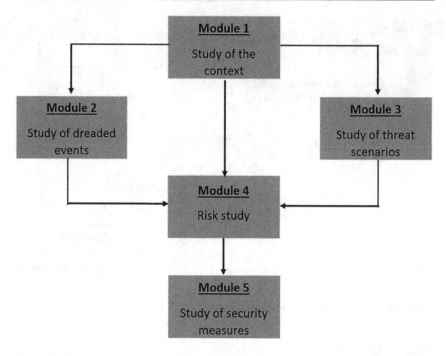

Figure 4.4 Iterative approach of the EBIOS method

- The fifth module, Study of Security Measures, is responsible for select-ing security measures to mitigate identified risks, aligning with the security objectives established in previous modules. Furthermore, this module includes planning for the implementation and validation of the selected security measures.

4.5.2.3 ISO 27005

The ISO 27005 standard is an international framework outlining the funda-mentals of a risk management process. While it defines a risk management approach, it does not prescribe a specific method, allowing each organiza-tion to adopt its own methodology. Frequently, the ISO standard references the EBIOS method. As illustrated in Figure 4.5, the ISO 27005 standard proposes a process structured into four primary phases:

- **Establishing the context:** This phase involves utilizing a detailed ques-tionnaire and conducting a preliminary study of the organization's context and its IS.
- **Risk assessment:** This phase encompasses analyzing and evaluating risks based on the organization's specific challenges.

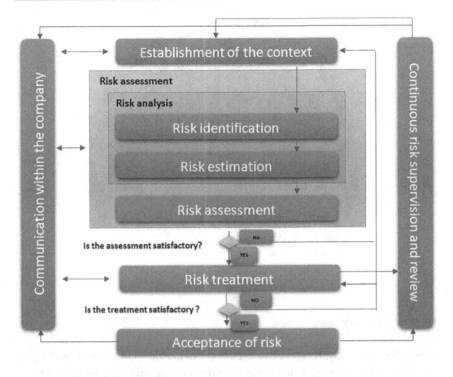

Figure 4.5 Process of ISO 27005 standard

- **Risk treatment:** During this phase, security measures are implemented to mitigate identified risks.
- **Acceptance of risk after treatment:** Following risk treatment, this phase involves accepting any residual risks.

In addition to these four phases, two other activities are conducted: communication within the company and supervision and continuous review of risk.

4.5.2.4 PDCA approach

The role of the PDCA approach is to ensure the effectiveness of the IS security policy and to deal with new malware and attacks, and it is necessary to follow a continuous improvement approach (Figure 4.6). The PDCA approach, often called the Deming Wheel, is the acronym for Plan, Do, Check, and Act.

The PDCA approach consists of continuously carrying out the following four steps:

- **Plan:** It consists of developing an IS security policy. This action is finalized by a reference document and an action plan.

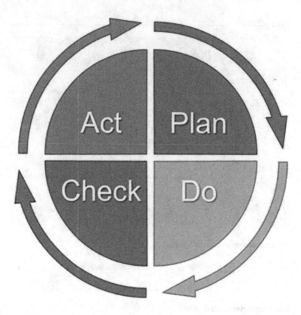

Figure 4.6 Deming Wheel

- **Develop (Do):** It refers to executing the action plan defined in the previous step through the implementation of security measures, employee awareness and training, etc.
- **Check:** It consists of carrying out recurring internal audits and controls in order to verify the effectiveness of the actions carried out during the previous stage, in particular the security measures put in place. The identification of one or more ineffective actions calls for making adjustments which will be defined and planned during the following step.
- **Adjust (Act):** It consists of implementing corrective actions for certain ineffective actions detected in the previous step, which do not require planning, or suggesting improvements for certain actions that will be planned in the step plan.

4.6 CONCLUSION

Threat modeling and risk management are proving to be indispensable pillars in the protection of systems and data in the field of cybersecurity. While threat modeling helps identify and assess specific vulnerabilities in a system, risk management provides a methodological framework for anticipating, assessing, and mitigating potential threats. By combining these two practices in an integrated manner, organizations can take a proactive and holistic approach to strengthening their security posture. The importance of this integration lies in the ability to anticipate threats, prioritize risks, and implement appropriate security measures. Thus, by embracing threat modeling and risk management as continuous and interdependent processes, organizations can better protect their assets and information, ensuring lasting security in an ever-changing environment.

REFERENCES

[1] S. Rizvi, R. Pipetti, N. McIntyre, J. Todd, and I. Williams, "Threat model for securing Internet of Things (IoT) network at device-level," Internet of Things, vol. 11, 2020, p. 100240.

[2] A. Motosho, B. Ayemlo Haruna, and O. Mikail Olaniyi, "Threat modeling of Internet of Things health devices," Journal of Applied Security Research, vol. 14, no. 1, 2019, pp. 106–121.

[3] M. Ouaissa, and M. Ouaissa, "Cyber security issues for IoT based smart grid infrastructure," IOP Conference Series: Materials Science and Engineering, vol. 937, no. 1, 2020, p. 012001.

[4] M. Cagnazzo, M. Hertlein, T. Holz, and N. Pohlmann, "Threat modeling for mobile health systems," In 2018 IEEE Wireless Communications and Networking Conference Workshops (WCNCW), pp. 314–319. New York: IEEE, 2018.

[5] S. G. Abbas, I. Vaccari, F. Hussain, S. Zahid, U. U. Fayyaz, G. A. Shah, G. A., T. Bakhshi, and E. Cambiaso, "Identifying and mitigating phishing attack threats in IoT use cases using a threat modelling approach," Sensors, vol. 21, no. 14, 2021, p. 4816.

[6] S. Raja, S. S. Manikandasaran, and R. Doss, "Threat modeling and IoT attack surfaces," In Immersive Technology in Smart Cities: Augmented and Virtual Reality in IoT. Gewerbestrasse, Switzerland: Springer, 2022, pp. 229–258.

[7] M. Mahak, and Y. Singh, "Threat modelling and risk assessment in Internet of Things: A review," In Proceedings of Second International Conference on Computing, Communications, and Cyber-Security: IC4S 2020, pp. 293–305. Singapore: Springer, 2021.

[8] S. G. Abbas, S. Zahid, F. Hussain, G. A. Shah, and M. Husnain, "A threat modelling approach to analyze and mitigate botnet attacks in smart home use case," In 2020 IEEE 14th International Conference on Big Data Science and Engineering (BigDataSE), pp. 122–129. New York: IEEE, 2020.

[9] Z. Abuabed, A. Alsadeh, and A. Taweel, "STRIDE threat model-based framework for assessing the vulnerabilities of modern vehicles," Computers & Security, vol. 133, 2023, p. 103391.

[10] M. R. Al Asif, K. F. Hasan, M. Z. Islam, and R. Khondoker, "STRIDE-based cyber security threat modeling for IoT-enabled precision agriculture systems," In 2021 3rd International Conference on Sustainable Technologies for Industry 4.0 (STI), pp. 1–6. New York: IEEE, 2021.

[11] L. Zhang, A. Taal, R. Cushing, C. de Laat, and P. Grosso, "A risk-level assessment system based on the STRIDE/DREAD model for digital data marketplaces," International Journal of Information Security, 2022, pp. 1–17.

[12] M. N. Alraja, U. J. Butt, and M. Abbod, "Information security policies compliance in a global setting: An employee's perspective," Computers & Security, vol. 129, 2023, p. 103208.

[13] M. Kamariotou, and F. Kitsios, "Information systems strategy and security policy: A conceptual framework," Electronics, vol. 12, no. 2, 2023, p. 382.

[14] L. G. Ording, S. Gao, and W. Chen, "The influence of inputs in the information security policy development: An institutional perspective," Transforming Government: People, Process and Policy, vol. 16, no. 4, 2022, pp. 418–435.

[15] E. S. Damayanti, "Risk management: In an overview of literature review," Formosa Journal of Science and Technology, vol. 2, no. 4, 2023, pp. 1115–1122.

[16] T. Aven, "Risk assessment and risk management: Review of recent advances on their foundation," European Journal of Operational Research, vol. 253, no. 1, 2016, pp. 1–13.

Chapter 5

Cybersecurity incident response and digital forensics

5.1 INTRODUCTION

A cyber incident represents an event or series of events that compromises the cybersecurity of an IS or computer network, resulting in harmful consequences for a company. The challenge lies in accurately evaluating the significance of a cybersecurity event, as a simple alert can escalate into a disaster [1].

Incident response, sometimes known as cybersecurity incident response, encompasses an organization's procedures and technologies designed to detect and address cyber threats, security breaches, or cyberattacks. The primary goal of incident response is to prevent cyberattacks proactively and to mitigate the costs and operational disruptions resulting from those that do occur [2].

Ideally, organizations establish formal incident response plans (IRPs) that outline processes and technologies for identifying, containing, and resolving various types of cyberattacks. A well-structured IRP assists cybersecurity teams in promptly detecting and containing cyber threats, enabling faster recovery of affected systems, and reducing financial losses, regulatory penalties, and other associated expenses. Digital forensics and incident response are two distinct components. Digital investigation, on the one hand, represents a subset of forensic science that analyzes system data, user activities, and other digital evidence to determine if an attack is ongoing and identify its perpetrator. On the other hand, incident response describes the overall process deployed by a company to prevent, detect, contain, and block data compromises. Given the proliferation of endpoints and the rise in cyberattacks in general, digital forensics and incident response have become central functionalities of companies' security and threat hunting strategies [3].

This chapter discusses strategies and techniques for managing cybersecurity incidents and conducting digital investigations. It covers the key steps of incident response and examines digital forensic methods for collecting, analyzing, and preserving electronic evidence, ensuring its integrity for forensic investigations. The objective is to minimize the impacts of security incidents and strengthen the resilience of IT systems. This chapter is organized into the following sections. In Section 5.2, we propose an overview of cybersecurity

DOI: 10.1201/9781003509080-5

incident response. Section 5.3 presents the impact of digital forensics in incident response. Section 5.4 describes the tools of digital forensics. We conclude in Section 5.5.

5.2 OVERVIEW OF CYBERSECURITY INCIDENT RESPONSE

5.2.1 Impact of security incident

5.2.1.1 Security incident

A security incident is an occurrence or event that compromises the proper functioning or security of an IS, or involves the unauthorized modification or destruction of information. In other words, it encompasses any intentional or unintentional incident that poses an increased threat to IT security. This could be a suspected, attempted, successful, or imminent threat of unauthorized access [4]. Regardless of the success or severity of the security incident, performing tracing and tracking procedures is paramount to ensuring the confidentiality and reliability of IT systems and preventing a recurrence in the future. A security incident may be isolated or consists of multiple events that together indicate that an organization's systems or data may have been compromised or that protective measures may have failed.

Some prevalent security incidents include:

- **Ransomware:** It is a type of malware that encrypts a victim's data or device, demanding a ransom payment to restore access.
- **Phishing and social engineering:** It attempts through digital or voice messages to deceive recipients into revealing sensitive information, downloading malware, or transferring funds to unauthorized entities.
- **DDoS attacks:** Hackers commandeer a large number of computers to flood a target organization's network or servers with traffic, rendering them inaccessible to legitimate users.
- **Supply chain attacks:** They are cyberattacks targeting an organization by exploiting vulnerabilities in its suppliers' systems or services, such as stealing data or distributing malware.
- **Insider threats:** Malicious insiders, including employees or partners, deliberately compromise an organization's security. Negligent insiders unintentionally breach security by disregarding best practices like using weak passwords or mishandling sensitive data.

5.2.1.2 Impacts of incidents

The impacts of security breaches encompass both immediate and lasting effects on individuals and organizations [5]:

- **Data loss:** Data may be destroyed or modified beyond recovery.
- **Damage to public image:** Good reputations are difficult to cultivate but easy to destroy.
- **Reduction in productivity:**
  - Productivity is defined as how well an employee does their job.
  - Employees must react and recover from the attack.
  - Attacked systems may experience downtime, rendering them unavailable. Consequently:
    - Employees cannot use the system.
    - Customers cannot use the system.
- **Legal action:**
  - Failing to properly protect personal information can result in heavy fines under data protection law.
  - Affected victims can sue the organization for compensation.

5.2.1.3 Cyber kill chain

A significant challenge for organizations is the rise of targeted attacks orchestrated by adversaries equipped with advanced tools and technologies. Their objective is to infiltrate the targeted cyber infrastructure stealthily and persistently. These attacks, often multistaged and intricate, entail vertical and horizontal maneuvers across various components of the organization. The security research community has termed this sequential progression of events culminating in cyber espionage as the cyber kill chain [6].

The cyber kill chain is essentially a cybersecurity model created by Lockheed Martin that outlines the steps of a cyberattack, identifies vulnerabilities, and assists security teams in halting attacks at each step in the chain. The term "kill chain" is adopted from the military, which uses it to describe the structure of an attack. It involves identifying a target, sending, deciding, ordering, and ultimately destroying the target.

5.2.1.4 Phases of kill chain

Developed by Lockheed Martin, the cyber kill chain framework is integral to the intelligence driven defense model, aimed at identifying and preventing cyber intrusion activities. This model delineates what adversaries must accomplish to achieve their objectives.

The cyber kill chain comprises seven steps that enhance visibility into an attack and deepen an analyst's comprehension of an adversary's TTP (Figure 5.1).

- Reconnaissance
  Like any form of traditional warfare, the most successful cyberattacks begin with a detailed search for information. Reconnaissance is the

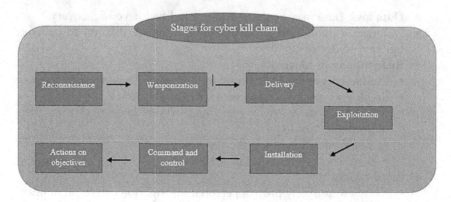

Figure 5.1 Stages of cyber kill chain

first step in the cyber kill chain. It employs various techniques and tools, as well as common web browsing functions.

- Weaponization
  Once a hacker has gathered sufficient information about their target, they select one or more attack vectors to initiate their intrusion. An attack vector refers to the method a hacker employs to gain unauthorized access to systems and information. These vectors vary from simple to highly technical approaches. However, it is essential to recognize that cybercriminals often choose targets based on evaluating the cost versus the potential return on investment (ROI) of their attacks.

- Delivery
  Once a hacker has breached your systems, they have the liberty to deploy any payload they possess, such as malware, ransomware, and spyware. They can install programs designed for different types of attacks, whether immediate, delayed, or triggered by specific actions (like logic bomb attacks). These assaults can be one-off occurrences, or hackers may remotely connect to your network to perpetually monitor and manage it.

- Exploitation
  After delivering the hacker's intended payload, the exploitation of the system commences contingent upon the type of attack. As mentioned earlier, some attacks are delayed, while others rely on specific actions by the target termed "logic bombs." These programs may incorporate masking functions to hide their activity and source, evading detection. Once the executable program is activated, the hacker can initiate the attack as intended, resulting in various forms of exploitation.

- Installation
  If a hacker identifies future attack opportunities, their subsequent action may involve installing a backdoor to secure permanent access

to the target's systems. This enables them to enter and exit the network without the risk of detection upon subsequent entries by other attack vectors. Backdoors can be established through methods such as rootkits and exploiting weak credentials. As long as their activity does not trigger suspicion from the security team, such as unusual login patterns or significant data transfers, it is challenging to identify these intrusions.

- Command and control
  After installing programs and backdoors, the hacker will take control of the systems and launch the attacks they have planned. All actions taken at this stage aim to maintain control over the target, which can involve planting ransomware, spyware, or other methods for future data exfiltration. Unfortunately, by the time you become aware of an intrusion and exfiltration, it is probably too late: the hackers have already taken control of your system. This is why it is crucial to have safeguards in place that monitor and evaluate data movements to detect suspicious activity. A machine can detect and prevent malicious behavior more quickly than any network administrator.
- Actions on objectives
  All these efforts have been undertaken to reach this point. During this continuous execution stage, the hacker acts on their target and can encrypt your data to obtain a ransom, exfiltrate your data for profit, disrupt your network via a DoS, or monitor the behavior of your system to detect further breaches via spyware, among other potential threats. Spying and surveillance are the primary actions in this final stage of the kill chain, during which attackers maintain a low profile and persist. This is where real-time monitoring of data movements and detection of suspicious behavior are crucial, as hackers will act swiftly to achieve their goals. There is never enough time to react to all possible anomalies within a large company. Therefore, your prevention efforts must be proactive rather than reactive.

5.2.2 Incident response planning

Cyberattacks usually start small and then snowball. Unfortunately, too few companies have adequate resources or processes to mitigate these threats before they grow. Since nothing prevents these cyberattacks from escalating from minor incidents to major risks for your business, they can have devastating consequences. Research shows that it takes an average of 128 days for businesses to detect a breach, providing hackers with four months to steal data, damage systems, and disrupt business operations.

Security incident response (SIR) is designed to help businesses respond to these types of network intrusions before they impact operations. Structured to manage various cyber threats and security incidents, SIR establishes reliable and scalable workflows and procedures that SOCs and incident response teams can use to minimize business impacts and reduce restoration times.

An organization's incident response is orchestrated through an IRP, usually crafted and executed by a Computer Security Incident Response Team (CSIRT). This team consists of stakeholders from various departments, including the CISO, SOC, IT staff, senior management, legal, human resources, regulatory compliance, and risk management.

A typical IRP includes:

- Clearly defined roles and responsibilities for each CSIRT member.
- Deployment of security solutions, including software, hardware, and other technologies, across the organization.
- Business continuity procedures outlining the steps for swiftly restoring critical systems and data following a failure.
- A comprehensive incident response methodology, detailing specific actions to be taken at each phase of the response process and assigning responsibilities.
- A communication strategy for notifying company management, employees, customers, and law enforcement agencies about incidents.
- Guidelines for documenting incident information for post-incident analysis and potential legal proceedings.

CSIRTs often develop separate IRPs tailored to different types of incidents, as each may demand a unique approach. Many organizations have specific plans for DDoS attacks, malware and ransomware incidents, and phishing attempts, with nearly half also having plans for addressing internal threats.

Some organizations enhance their internal CSIRT capabilities by partnering with external firms offering incident response services. These partners, usually engaged on a contractual basis, provide support in various aspects of incident management, including plan preparation and execution.

5.2.3 Incident response life cycle

Most IRPs adhere to a standardized incident response framework developed by organizations such as the SANS Institute, the NIST, and the Cybersecurity and Infrastructure Agency (CISA). Here is a breakdown of the general incident response phases:

- Preparation
  This phase involves ongoing activities to ensure the CSIRT is equipped with the necessary procedures and tools to respond swiftly and effectively to incidents while minimizing disruptions. Regular risk assessments help identify network vulnerabilities and prioritize potential

security incidents based on their impact. IRPs are updated or created accordingly.

- **Detection and analysis**
  During this phase, security teams monitor the network for suspicious activity and analyze data from various sources, such as device logs and security tools like antivirus software and firewalls. Security solutions like SIEM and EDR aid in real-time event monitoring and automated incident detection. The communication plan is activated to notify relevant personnel upon identifying the type of threat or breach.
- **Containment**
  The CSIRT takes immediate action to prevent the breach from spreading further. Short-term containment involves isolating affected systems, while long-term measures focus on strengthening security controls to protect unaffected systems. Backups are created to prevent data loss, and forensic evidence is collected for analysis.
- **Eradication**
  Once the threat is contained, the team proceeds with removing the threat from the system entirely. This includes eliminating malware and unauthorized users and verifying the integrity of affected systems.
- **Recovery**
  With the threat eradicated, the CSIRT restores affected systems to normal operation. This involves deploying patches, rebuilding systems from backups, and bringing devices back online.
- **Post-Incident review**
  The CSIRT conducts a comprehensive review of the incident, analyzing collected evidence to understand its root cause and how it breached the network. Vulnerabilities are addressed to prevent similar incidents in the future.

5.2.4 Incident response technologies

As mentioned earlier, IRPs not only outline the actions CSIRTs need to take during a security incident but also detail the necessary security solutions for executing or automating key incident response workflows, including collecting and correlating security data, detecting real-time incidents, and responding to ongoing attacks.

Here are some of the commonly used incident response technologies:

- **Security information and event management**: SIEM platforms aggregate and correlate security event data from various internal security tools and network devices. They help combat "alert fatigue" by identifying real threats among the high volume of notifications generated by these tools.

- **Security orchestration, automation, and response:** SOAR platforms enable security teams to define formalized workflows, known as playbooks, that coordinate different operations and security tools in response to incidents. These workflows can automate certain tasks to improve efficiency.
- **Endpoint detection and response:** EDR software protects an organization's end users, endpoints, and IT assets from cyber threats that evade traditional security tools. It continuously collects and analyzes data from network endpoints in real time to detect and respond to known or suspected threats.
- **Extended detection and response:** XDR solutions unify security tools, data sources, and analytics across hybrid IT environments to create a centralized system for threat prevention, detection, and response. By eliminating tool silos and automating responses, XDR streamlines security operations.
- **User and entity behavior analytics (UEBA):** UEBA utilizes behavioral analytics, ML, and automation to identify anomalous user and device behavior that may indicate security threats. It is effective at detecting insider threats and compromised internal credentials.
- **Attack surface management (ASM):** ASM solutions automate the discovery, analysis, remediation, and monitoring of vulnerabilities and potential attack vectors across an organization's attack surface. They identify previously unmonitored network assets and enhance overall security posture by mapping relationships between assets.

5.3 DIGITAL FORENSICS IN INCIDENT RESPONSE

5.3.1 How SIEM works

To identify and investigate security incidents, many companies rely on SOC. The SOC is a team dedicated to supervising the security of the IS. To do this, it uses monitoring tools, as well as tools for collection, remote intervention, and event correlation. It looks for signs of an incident or compromise, such as weak signals or abnormal behavior, to protect the IS. This monitoring helps detect security events like intrusions, unauthorized code execution, exploits, privilege escalation, and attempted access to admin accounts. The SOC is therefore a crucial element for the security of company data.

To manage alerts and detect intrusions, SOC teams use a SIEM system. It is one of the central tools for monitoring security that we will explore in more detail in the next parts of this course. The main mission of a SOC is to identify, analyze, and remedy cybersecurity incidents through the monitoring of various equipment, as well as analysis and monitoring methods.

Setting up a SOC can be complicated and expensive. However, it is an investment that should not be overlooked to protect company data and to respond quickly in the event of a compromise. The centralization of logs allows for more organized investigations, aimed at finding the sources and vectors of an attack in the event of an incident. SOCs monitor and administer the security of the IS to identify, analyze, and remedy security incidents.

The benefits of a SOC include the protection of sensitive data and compliance with industry regulations. It is also suitable for deploying and implementing solutions for detection and analysis, such as log collection servers, IPS/IDS, EDR systems, and a SIEM.

SIEM is an approach to security management that provides security professionals with insight and a historical record of activities within their IT environment. It generates alerts based on the analysis and correlation of multiple security event sources. SIEM technology has been around for over a decade, evolving initially from the discipline of log management. It combines:

- **Security event management (SEM):** This technology analyzes log and event data in real time to offer threat monitoring, event correlation, and incident response capabilities.
- **Security information management (SIM):** SIM solutions collect, analyze, and report on log data.
  SIEM combines both SEM and SIM functionalities. It collects and aggregates log data generated across an organization's IS, spanning from applications to network and security devices like firewalls and anti-malware systems. SIEM then identifies and categorizes incidents and events before analyzing them. This software serves two primary objectives:
- **Provide reporting on security incidents and events:** This entails generating reports on various security-related activities, such as successful and failed login attempts, malware detections, and other potentially malicious activities.
- **Send alerts:** If the analysis shows that an activity matches predetermined rule sets, such as the execution of malware, it indicates a potential security issue.

5.3.2 Digital forensics

5.3.2.1 Digital forensic principle

Forensic analysis, or digital forensics, involves analyzing an infected machine to understand what happened and to prepare a report with the conclusions of the analysis and recommendations. Forensic analysis relies on a set of techniques and tools for researching, collecting, and analyzing data to find and interpret information (traces) left on a machine. The main objective is to understand where an attack comes from and how it operates [7]. Forensic analysis is based on two main points:

- **Searching for traces on the Internet:** This involves studying a malicious site to find information about its owner, such as their email address or geographical position.
- **Searching for local traces:** This involves conducting a digital investigation on a machine by examining Windows log files, for example, to find traces of deleted files. The goal is to reproduce the "timeline" of the machine's usage.

5.3.2.2 Objectives of digital forensics

- **Recover, analyze, and preserve evidence:** It ensures that computers and related materials are handled in a way that allows them to be presented as evidence in court.
- **Determine motive and culprit identity:** It helps identify the reason behind the crime and the main perpetrator.
- **Design procedures for crime scenes:** It establishes methods at suspected crime scenes to ensure that digital evidence is not corrupted.
- **Data acquisition and duplication:** This process involves retrieving deleted files and partitions from digital media to extract and validate evidence.
- **Identify evidence quickly:** It enables rapid identification of evidence and helps estimate the potential impact of malicious activity on the victim.
- **Produce an IT expert report:** It provides a comprehensive report on the investigation process.
- **Preserve evidence:** It ensures the integrity of evidence by following the chain of custody.

5.3.2.3 Types of digital forensics

- **Disk forensics:** It involves obtaining evidence from digital storage media such as USB devices, DVDs, and CDs by gathering active files or modifying or deleting the files.
- **Network forensics:** It is a subpart of digital forensics that involves monitoring and detecting system network traffic to extract crucial data for legal evidence to be presented in court.
- **Wireless forensics:** It is a subset of network forensics that focuses on collecting and extracting evidence from wireless network traffic.
- **Database forensics:** It involves the study and collection of databases and their relevant metadata. It uses investigative techniques to query the database and collect evidence.

- **Malware forensics:** It focuses on identifying malicious codes and studying issues related to their operation, such as Trojans, viruses, and other types of malware.
- **Email forensics:** It deals with the recovery and analysis of email data, including deleted emails, calendar entries, and contact information.
- **Memory analysis:** It involves collecting data from the computer's cache or RAM and gathering evidence from that memory.

5.3.2.4 Importance of digital forensics in incident response

Although digital forensics and incident response have traditionally been reactive security functions, the sophisticated tools and advanced technologies now available, such as AI and ML, have enabled some businesses to leverage these operations to influence and document preventative measures. In this case, digital forensics and incident response can also be considered key components of a proactive security strategy [8].

Digital forensics provides the information and evidence that the IT Emergency Response Team or IT SIR Team needs to respond to a security incident. Digital investigation can cover different aspects:

- **File system investigation:** It scans endpoint file systems for signs of compromise.
- **Memory investigation:** It scans memory for attack indicators that may not be present in the file system.
- **Network investigation:** It analyzes network activity, including email, chat, and Internet browsing, to identify attacks, understand the attack techniques used, and determine the scale of the incident.
- **Log analysis:** It analyzes and interprets records or activity logs to identify any suspicious activity or unusual events.

In addition to providing valuable assistance to teams responsible for responding to attacks, digital forensics plays a key role in the remediation process. It can also provide the necessary evidence for the resolution of disputes or useful documentation for auditors. Furthermore, the analysis carried out by the digital forensics team can be very useful in defining and strengthening preventative security measures, helping companies reduce overall risk and improve their future response times.

Although digital forensics and incident response are two distinct functions, they are closely related and, in some ways, interdependent. Integrating digital forensics and incident response offers businesses several major benefits, including:

- Fast and accurate response to incidents.
- Consistent processes for investigating and evaluating incidents.

- Reduction of data loss or theft, as well as reputational damage resulting from a cyberattack.
- Strengthening existing security protocols and procedures through a better understanding of the threat and risk landscape.
- Faster recovery of activities after a security incident and limited disruption of operations.
- Collection of evidence and documentation useful for prosecuting cybercriminals.

5.3.3 Phases of digital forensics in incident response

By adhering to the following steps, forensic professionals can provide clear and comprehensive insights into the nature and source of cyberattacks, facilitating effective response and remediation [9] (Figure 5.2).

- **Identification**
  This is the first step in the forensic process. It involves determining what evidence is present, where it is stored, and in what format. Electronic storage media can include personal computers, mobile phones, tablets, and more.
- **Preservation**
  In this phase, data is isolated, secured, and preserved. This involves preventing unauthorized access to the digital device to ensure that digital evidence remains intact and unaltered.

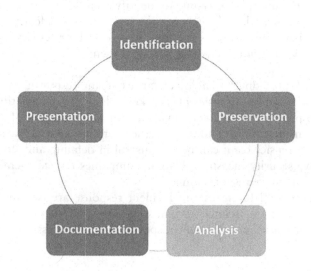

Figure 5.2 Phases of digital forensics

- **Analysis**
  During this stage, investigative agents analyze fragments of data and draw conclusions based on the evidence discovered. Multiple iterations of examination may be necessary to support a particular criminal theory.
- **Documentation**
  This process involves creating a record of all visible data to allow for its recreation during examination. Proper documentation of the crime scene is essential, including taking photographs, making sketches, and mapping the crime scene.
- **Presentation**
  The final step involves summarizing and explaining the findings. The report must be written in simple terms, with abstract terminologies clearly explained and referring to specific details.

5.3.4 Analysis techniques of digital forensics

5.3.4.1 Indicators of compromise

Indicators of compromise (IoCs) are crucial elements discovered during the analysis of cyber incidents. They help characterize the incident and identify threats, providing essential data for mitigating and responding to attacks. IoCs can be of various types, each offering unique insights into malicious activities. Understanding these indicators is key to enhancing network security and incident response capabilities [10].

- **Network IoCs**: These refer to malicious network activities, such as connections to a C2 server. Identifying these indicators enables quick action to block harmful connections that contain threats across the network. Analyzing network frames generated by malware helps create IDS rules to proactively detect intrusions or malicious connections. Domain names and URLs also fall under this category.
- **File hashes**: Hashes are unique fingerprints that identify files. Malicious files on a machine can be identified using their hashes, making it easier to detect and remove threats. Additionally, identifying the directories where these malicious files are stored helps in thorough system cleanup.
- **Email addresses**: Addresses used for delivering spam, phishing, or other malicious emails are also IoCs. Blocking these addresses on email gateways can prevent further malicious emails from reaching users.
- **System actions**: Actions performed by malware on a system can be significant IoCs. For example, the creation of specific Windows services or registry keys by malware can indicate a compromise. Identifying these actions helps in understanding the behavior of the malware and taking appropriate remediation steps.

By identifying and understanding various IoCs, organizations can better protect their systems, detect threats early, and respond effectively to cyber incidents.

5.3.4.2 MITRE ATT&CK matrix

The ATT&CK matrix is an initiative by MITRE which helps identify the tactics and techniques used by attackers. It provides a set of classifications to identify the different phases of an attack, as well as the techniques used for each phase [11].

The objectives of using the matrix for your information security are multifaceted:

- Conduct an analysis of your detection capabilities and identify weaknesses proactively.
- Improve your threat detection and investigation methodology.
- Test your detection rules to ensure you are alerted as expected.
- **Tactics**
  An attacker's strategic objective may be to extort money through ransom, steal information, or simply destroy an organization's IT environment. To achieve these objectives, attackers implement a series of progressive actions, known as tactics. The different stages of an attack typically include:
  - **Initial access**: This phase defines the techniques used by an attacker to gain access to the target network, such as through a phishing attack.
  - **Execution**: This phase identifies the techniques used to enable code execution within the target environment.
  - **Persistence**: This phase defines the techniques used to allow an attacker to maintain continued access to a compromised system.
  - **Privilege escalation**: This phase defines the means used by an attacker to obtain higher privileges on target machines.
  - **Defense evasion**: This phase identifies the methods used to circumvent security solutions and protections put in place.
  - **Credential access**: This phase represents a collection of techniques used to gain access to or control system, domain, or service credentials within an enterprise environment. Adversaries frequently acquire legitimate credentials from users or administrator accounts, such as local system administrators or domain users with administrator access, for use on the network.
  - **Discovery**: This phase involves techniques aimed at acquiring knowledge about the system and internal network. When attackers gain access to a new system, they must understand its architecture and functionality.

- **Lateral movement:** This phase consists of techniques that allow an attacker to access and control remote systems on a network. It may include running tools on these remote systems. Lateral movement techniques could allow an adversary to collect information from a system without the need for additional tools, such as a remote access tool.
- **Collection:** This phase consists of techniques for identifying and gathering information, such as sensitive files, from a target network before exfiltration. This category also covers locations on a system or network where the adversary can search for information to exfiltrate data.
- **Command and control:** This phase shows how adversaries communicate with systems under their control within a target network. An adversary can establish command and control in different ways, depending on the system configuration and network topology. Due to the wide degree of variation available to the adversary at the network level, only the most common factors were used to describe command and control differences. The documented methods still contain many specific techniques, largely due to the ease with which it is possible to define new protocols and use existing legitimate network protocols and services for communication.
- **Exfiltration:** This phase consists of techniques for stealing, altering, or deleting data. The attacker may use techniques to hide these actions, making it difficult to determine if they actually occurred. The attacker had access to all the files on the compromised machine and potentially deleted, altered, or stole information.
- **Impact:** This phase represents techniques whose primary objective is to directly reduce the availability or integrity of a system, service, or network. This includes the manipulation of data to impact an activity or operational process. These techniques may represent the adversary's end goal or provide cover in the event of a privacy violation.

It is important to understand that tactics are classifications and descriptions of modes of operation. Tactics describe what the attacker is trying to do at any stage of the attack and do not necessarily follow a defined order.

- **Techniques**

While tactics specify what the attacker is trying to achieve, techniques describe the various methods attackers develop to carry out a tactic. For example, if attackers aim to maintain access to a compromised IS, they employ the persistence tactic. This tactic can be executed in several ways, as listed under techniques. Attackers might create a RUN registry key or set up a malicious service that allows the execution of malicious software on each reboot or at a given time.

Techniques with the same objective are grouped under the same tactic. For each technique, the matrix provides examples of known cases where the technique is:

- Used by a group of attackers.
- Implemented by malicious software.

All this information helps you to precisely identify the techniques used, allowing you to thoroughly adjust your supervision and detection mechanisms.

5.3.4.3 Threat hunting

- **Characteristics of threat hunting**

Having solidified endpoint security and incident response strategies to mitigate known malware attacks, such as APTs, security experts can then go on the offensive. They are ready to dig deep and find what has not yet been detected. This is exactly the goal of threat hunting [12].

Threat hunting can be defined as a proactive strategy designed to find unknown threats or hidden adversaries inside a network before they can execute an attack or achieve their objectives. It involves an investigative method of testing an evolving set of hypotheses using threat hunting toolkits that enable both creative detective work and workflows based on new discoveries.

The goal of threat hunting is to monitor the daily activities of a system and network traffic, looking for any anomalies to detect malicious activity that has successfully bypassed an organization's defenses and could lead to a partial or complete breach. Unlike most security techniques, threat hunting goes further to find evasive bad actors. It combines the capabilities and data of an advanced security solution with the strong analytical and technical skills of an individual or a team of threat hunting professionals [13].

- **Threat hunting methodologies**

Threat hunting experts assume that an attacker is already in the network. They look for IoC, lateral movement, and other telltale artifacts that can provide evidence of attack behavior [14].

Depending on the research starting point, threat hunting can follow one of the following three methodologies or techniques:

- **Hypothesis hunting**: This methodology consists of testing three types of hypotheses:
  - Analytics-driven: It uses user behavior analysis and ML to develop aggregated risk scores and formulate hypotheses.

- Intelligence-driven: It includes intelligence feed analysis, vulnerability scans, malware analysis, and reporting.
- Situational awareness: It involves risk assessments and identification of digital assets critical to the business or organization to secure.
- **Structured hunting**: This is the most proactive threat hunting methodology. The tasks that occur most often in this methodology are:
  - Using indicators of attack (IoA) and TTP to determine threat actors.
  - Estimating the environment, domain, and attack behaviors to create a hypothesis that aligns with the MITRE ATT&CK framework (MAF).
  - Specifying a behavior and attempting to locate threat patterns by monitoring activities on the system.
- **Unstructured hunting**: This begins from a trigger or indicator of compromise. This type of threat hunting can uncover new types of threats or threats that have entered the environment in the past and are now dormant. The threat hunter scans the network for malicious patterns before and after the trigger or IoC. The hunter can investigate historical data to the extent that data backup limits allow.
- **Identification of steps**

Creating an effective threat hunting program is among the top priorities for security leaders looking to become more proactive and implement active defenses [15].

A proactive threat hunting process typically includes three stages: an initial trigger stage, followed by a thorough investigation and ending with resolution (Figure 5.3).

- **Step 1: Trigger**
  Threat hunting is generally a targeted process. Initially, the hunter gathers information about the targeted environment and then develops hypotheses about potential threats. A threat hunter can use information about current threats or TTPs from attackers, in addition to their knowledge, experience, and creative problem-solving skills, to establish a threat hypothesis and decide on the path forward.

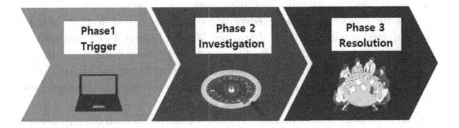

Figure 5.3 Phases of threat hunting

Next, the hunter chooses a trigger, typically identified in a specific application or area of the network, for further investigation. A hypothesis can serve as a trigger when advanced detection tools prompt threat hunters to launch an investigation into a particular system or a specific area of a network.

- **Step 2: Investigation**
  Once a trigger is chosen, threat hunters look deeply for potentially malicious anomalies in the system or network. During the investigation, threat hunters use a wide range of technologies and tools, such as UEBA and SIEM, to help them investigate anomalies, which may or may not be malicious. The investigation continues until the hypothesis is either proven or disproven.
- **Step 3: Resolution**
  During the remediation stage, information collected during the preceding stage is communicated to security and operations teams to quickly respond and mitigate threats. Actions to take may include:
  - Updating firewall and IPS rules
  - Restoration of modified files
  - Deletion of malicious files
  - Changing system configurations
  - Deployment of security patches
  - Documentation of attacker methods

5.4 TOOLS OF DIGITAL FORENSICS

To carry out a forensic analysis of digital media, there are recognized tools on the market [16]:

- **Guidance Software Encase**: This suite of utilities is dedicated to forensic analysis, covering disk analysis, data sorting, file analysis, and decryption of analyzed volumes. Although Encase licenses require payment and are relatively expensive, this type of tool is widely used by legal experts and police organizations.
- **Write blockers**: These hardware tools allow the collection of digital media without data alteration. Write blockers block the writing mechanism but not the reading mechanism, preserving the content's integrity. A hardware write blocker is placed between the hard drive (the evidence) and the PC used to acquire the image. There are also software write blockers available.
- **Free or open source utilities**: These are commonly used during forensic analyses.

- **The Sleuth Kit**: This framework facilitates forensic analysis by generating timelines, sorting data, and analyzing Windows artifacts (registry, email, history, etc.), and includes a GUI called Autopsy.
- **NirSoft Utilities and Microsoft's Sysinternals Suite**: These tools are also used in forensic analysis.
- **Google Rapid Response (GRR)**: Developed by Google, this framework allows remote forensic analysis of compromised workstations.
- **Linux OS for forensic analysis**: Some projects offer Linux operating systems intended for forensic analysis, with preinstalled tools such as:
  - **SANS Investigative Forensic Toolkit (SIFT)**
  - **Tsurugi**
  - **Computer Aided INvestigative Environment (CAINE)**
  - **Digital Evidence & Forensics Toolkit (DEFT)**
- **RAM Analysis Frameworks**: Tools such as Volatility and Rekall are used for analyzing RAM.
- **FTK Imager Lite**: This freeware can be used for copying hard drives and RAM.

These tools and utilities help forensic analysts perform comprehensive and accurate investigations by ensuring data integrity, enabling detailed analysis, and facilitating the generation of reports.

5.5 CONCLUSION

It is crucial for organizations to have robust strategies in place to manage security incidents and conduct effective digital investigations. The ability to quickly identify, investigate, and correct cyberattacks not only minimizes negative impacts on IS but also strengthens their resilience to future threats. Mastery of digital forensic techniques is essential for ensuring the collection and preservation of electronic evidence, thereby ensuring its validity in a judicial context. By developing these skills and taking a proactive approach, organizations can better protect their sensitive data and maintain the trust of their stakeholders.

REFERENCES

[1] M. Iaiani, A. Tugnoli, S. Bonvicini, and V. Cozzani, "Analysis of cybersecurity-related incidents in the process industry," Reliability Engineering & System Safety, vol. 209, 2021, p. 107485.

[2] M. Ouaissa, and M. Ouaissa, "Cyber security issues for IoT based smart grid infrastructure," IOP Conference Series: Materials Science and Engineering, vol. 937, no. 1, 2020, p. 012001.

[3] H. Naseer, S. B. Maynard, and K. C. Desouza, "Demystifying analytical information processing capability: The case of cybersecurity incident response," Decision Support Systems, vol. 143, 2021, p. 113476.

[4] A. Zamfiroiu, and R. C. Sharma, "Cybersecurity management for incident response," Romanian Cyber Security Journal, 2022, pp. 2668–6430.

[5] A. Naseer, H. Naseer, A. Ahmad, S. B. Maynard, and A. M. Siddiqui, "Moving towards agile cybersecurity incident response: A case study exploring the enabling role of big data analytics-embedded dynamic capabilities," Computers & Security, vol. 135, 2023, p. 103525.

[6] R. Kour, A. Thaduri, and R. Karim, "Railway defender kill chain to predict and detect cyber-attacks," Journal of Cyber Security and Mobility, vol. 9, no. 1, 2020, pp. 47–90.

[7] A. A. Khan, A. A. Shaikh, A. A. Laghari, M. A. Dootio, M. M. Rind, and S. A. Awan, "Digital forensics and cyber forensics investigation: Security challenges, limitations, open issues, and future direction," International Journal of Electronic Security and Digital Forensics, vol. 14, no. 2, 2022, pp. 124–150.

[8] M. I. Alghamdi, "Digital forensics in cyber security—recent trends, threats, and opportunities," Cybersecurity Threats with New Perspective, 2021.

[9] P. Binnar, and S. Bhirud, "Security analysis of cyber physical system using digital forensic incident response," Cyber Security and Applications, 2023, p. 100034.

[10] H. Dubey, S. Bhatt, and L. Negi, "Digital forensics techniques and trends: A review," The International Arab Journal of Information Technology (IAJIT), vol. 20, no. 4, 2023, pp. 644–654.

[11] W. Xiong, E. Legrand, O. Åberg, and R. Lagerström, "Cyber security threat modeling based on the MITRE Enterprise ATT&CK matrix," Software and Systems Modeling, vol. 21, no. 1, 2022, pp. 157–177.

[12] M. S. Khan, R. Richard, H. Molyneaux, D. Cote-Martel, H. J. K. Elango, S. Livingstone, M. Gaudet, and D. Trask, "Cyber threat hunting: A cognitive endpoint behavior analytic system," International Journal of Cognitive Informatics and Natural Intelligence (IJCINI), vol. 15, no. 4, 2021, pp. 1–23.

[13] T. Bikov, D. Radev, T. Iliev, and D. Stankovski, "Threat hunting as cyber security baseline in the next-generation security operations center," In 2021 29th Telecommunications Forum (TELFOR), pp. 1–4. New York: IEEE, 2021.

[14] M. S. Kulkarni, D. H. Ashit, and C. N. Chetan, "A proactive approach to advanced cyber threat hunting," In 2023 7th International Conference on Computation System and Information Technology for Sustainable Solutions (CSITSS), pp. 1–6. New York: IEEE, 2023.

[15] G. González-Granadillo, S. González-Zarzosa, and R. Diaz, "Security information and event management (SIEM): Analysis, trends, and usage in critical infrastructures," Sensors, vol. 21, no. 14, 2021, p. 4759.

[16] K. Touloumis, A. Michalitsi-Psarrou, A. Georgiadou, and D. Askounis, "A tool for assisting in the forensic investigation of cyber-security incidents," In 2022 IEEE International Conference on Big Data (Big Data), pp. 2630–2636. New York: IEEE, 2022.

Chapter 6

Use of AI and blockchain in cybersecurity

6.1 INTRODUCTION

Cybersecurity in the IoT is a critical area due to the rapid growth in the number of connected devices and their integration into vital aspects of daily life, such as smart homes, critical infrastructure, and healthcare [1]. AI and blockchain offer diverse approaches to threat detection. Although they possess distinct characteristics, their individual or combined capabilities hold significant promise for bolstering cybersecurity. Given the critical importance of cybersecurity in today's digital age, it is imperative to thwart evolving attack vectors [2]. Blockchain, with its decentralized and immutable nature, provides a robust solution to secure transactions and ensure data integrity, thereby eliminating risks associated with the manipulation and falsification of information. Together, these technologies provide an integrated, multi-faceted approach to cybersecurity, helping build more resilient and adaptive systems in the face of evolving threats [3].

However, implementing these technologies also presents challenges, including interoperability, managing the limited resources of IoT devices, and the complexity of security updates. Further research and development are crucial to overcoming these obstacles and maximizing the benefits offered by the convergence of AI, IoT, and blockchain. This chapter delves into how blockchain and AI can effectively mitigate cyber threats. The structure of this chapter is as follows. Section 6.2 provides an overview of AI in cybersecurity. Section 6.3 describes the concept and security in connected objects. In Section 6.4, we explain the role of blockchain in cybersecurity. Conclusions are drawn in Section 6.5.

6.2 AI IN CYBERSECURITY

AI aims to build computer programs that perform tasks requiring high-level mental processes such as perceptual learning, memory organization, and critical reasoning. In other words, it encompasses all the theoretical and

DOI: 10.1201/9781003509080-6

technical means for making machines simulate behaviors generally associated with human intelligence. Nowadays, work on AI aims to solve problems more effectively than human intelligence. The work and applications focus on narrow AI, dedicated to specific tasks such as content recommendation, image recognition for authentication or pathology detection, and automatic translation [4].

Various areas of research contribute to the general approach to creating AI, including knowledge representation, natural language processing, robotics, planning, and cognitive modeling. These research fields have been active for decades, but a significant resurgence of interest in AI, both academic and industrial, occurred in the early 2010s with the rapid development of big data, data sciences in general, and ML in particular (supervised or unsupervised), especially deep learning. It is therefore of great importance to protect AI against fraudulent use and to make comparable efforts in the cyber protection of AI as in the development of AI itself [5].

Several security flaws in commercial AI are regularly highlighted. The path seems marked for more serious attacks, such as access unlocking and money transfer. Using similar techniques, cybercriminals can target the AI controlling the authentication of a financial institution, or an unscrupulous company can target the AI defining the pricing strategy of its competitor [6].

These threats affect all stages of the implementation of AI. The ML methodology is based on three stages: data acquisition, learning from this database, and action based on new data. The resulting system is improved and corrected through an iterative process during execution. Each of these steps presents a risk of compromise.

- During the training data acquisition stage, the data can be corrupted or manipulated.
- During the learning stage, the learning algorithms can be misused or corrupted.
- During the system setup stage, the configuration of system components can be altered and diverted from their main objective.

This three-step methodology also presents two main security risks. The first is that systems are generally designed to run in a closed loop, without human intervention, in their daily work. Attacks on these systems can therefore remain undetected for a long time. The second risk relates to the large volume of data manipulated by AI algorithms, which makes the reasons guiding such decisions often difficult to interpret. This means that even if an attack is detected, the motivations behind it may remain opaque [7].

AI methodologies, technologies, and tools can also be used to protect systems from cyberattacks. An analysis of past cyberattacks can help differentiate truly dangerous situations from those that are less severe. More generally,

AI can help strengthen the security of AI-enabled systems during the three main stages of cybersecurity: attack prevention, detection, and response.

- **Prevention:** ML can be used to learn from previous attacks and implement relevant systems for each identified security threat. This forecasting system will be able to quickly adapt to previously unknown threats.
- **Detection:** Detection methods based on attack signatures are being enhanced with AI. AI-based algorithms can now detect any change from a situation defined as normal in the system, providing greater potential for identifying previously unknown threats. Furthermore, reinforcement learning and deep learning now make it possible to operate effectively without large training databases, becoming operational much more quickly in this attack detection context.
- **Response:** AI can greatly assist in responding to cyberattacks by prioritizing the work of analysts and directing them toward high value-added activities. It can also enable the automatic quarantine of parts of the system or its users during an attack.

6.3 CYBERSECURITY IN CONNECTED OBJECTS

New technologies often tend to overlook security, making them a perfect target for cybercriminals who use them as gateways to access connected networks and steal stored data.

6.3.1 IoT concept

The IoT has seen continued expansion, with a growing number of connected objects. This results in vulnerabilities that can have very critical impacts. Cybersecurity of the IoT represents a significant challenge. Once connected to the Internet, an object becomes capable of receiving and sending information. In a way, it becomes intelligent. Connecting to the cloud and the Internet allows an object to access data storage and computing resources of powerful servers, providing many possibilities [8].

As connected objects have a fairly short lifespan, consumers may assume that they are already secured by the manufacturer and may not apply the patches available to them if they have to do so manually. Connectivity is now an essential feature for various devices, not just smart gadgets. It is imperative for vehicles, medical devices, and industrial and telecommunications equipment. Consequently, these connected objects may also be subject to certain vulnerabilities [9].

In the early years of IoT, the lack of clear standards and regulatory frameworks made it difficult for manufacturers to develop an appropriate level of security assurance for their products. Today, there are multiple internationally recognized standards, frameworks, and certification programs that can help, including IEC 62443, ETSI EN 303 645, and ISO 21434.

IoT enables the extension of Internet connectivity beyond computers and smartphones, reaching almost all objects. IoT sensors facilitate the collection of various data and information. For instance, a sensor can measure temperature, humidity, movement, air quality, brightness, and more. When coupled with an Internet connection, this data can be analyzed to make informed decisions. For example, a farm can gather information on soil moisture to determine the optimal timing for watering plants, thereby preventing over or under watering. Similar to how our senses provide information about our environment, IoT sensors offer objects the ability to gather data. Computers then process this information from sensors.

This interconnectedness enables remote sensing and control of objects via existing network infrastructure, facilitating a seamless integration of the physical world into computing systems. This leads to enhanced efficiency and precision across multiple sectors. Initial IoT applications have emerged in fields such as healthcare, transportation, industry, and agriculture. Despite being in its early stages, IoT technology has made considerable strides in connecting objects with sensors to the Internet [10].

Additionally, IoT allows objects to receive data and instructions. For instance, in the context of a farm, an irrigation system connected to the Internet can be automatically activated if its humidity sensors detect that watering is necessary.

6.3.2 IoT and cybersecurity

The most significant vulnerability of the IoT is a severe cybersecurity issue. Protecting this vast attack surface is an immense challenge. For instance, hackers have exploited numerous obsolete connected objects to create botnets and launch DDoS attacks. Anything connected to the Internet is susceptible to hacking, and connected objects are no exception. A lack of security in IoT systems has resulted in data breaches from connected objects [11]. IoT devices are particularly vulnerable due to their limited storage and processing capacity, making it challenging to install antivirus software, firewalls, or other security measures. Nevertheless, they capture sufficient data to make them attractive targets for cybercriminals. Furthermore, IoT also introduces risks of espionage and surveillance.

6.3.3 Threats of IoT

Cyberattacks targeting the IoT are on the rise, particularly with the increasing trend of telecommuting [12].

DDoS attacks involve flooding a website's traffic, causing it to crash. They can also be utilized to overwhelm an IoT network, disrupting connected objects, or to enlist these objects into a "botnet" to launch further DDoS attacks.

Another significant threat is malware, capable of infecting connected objects much like computers or smartphones. Malware can disrupt operations, hijack devices, or steal data.

SQL code injection poses a risk to connected objects, allowing hackers to access and retrieve data. Additionally, hackers can identify IoT devices within Wi-Fi networks for potential attacks.

Zero-day vulnerabilities, present in devices straight from the factory, also pose significant risks. Finally, there is a concern for surveillance and espionage targeting connected objects.

6.3.4 Security solutions in IoT

To bolster IoT security, the implementation of universal standards is imperative. Connected objects need to communicate and share data efficiently, yet the current plethora of communication protocols is often incompatible. The adoption of standards will not only ensure IoT security but also foster the development of new products [13].

In navigating this technology, a cautious approach is essential. Various services, protocols, and solutions exist to tackle the challenge of IoT security. Organizations can lean on dedicated frameworks for IoT cybersecurity, such as those provided by NIST. Specifically, they should conduct vulnerability assessments for all connected devices and establish response plans for potential incidents.

Compartmentalizing IoT devices helps minimize the attack surface, and the addition of security software and devices creates virtual barriers. Continuous monitoring of threats is crucial, with immediate deployment of updates to address vulnerabilities. Furthermore, default passwords on IoT devices should be avoided.

Robust authentication systems and access controls are paramount, and data communications between IoT devices should be encrypted and secure. Regular data backups are essential to mitigate risks. New technologies like AI and ML, along with real-time analysis, can provide invaluable support.

Above all, comprehensive employee training in cybersecurity is paramount. Every individual within the organization must be vigilant, knowledgeable about existing threats, and capable of identifying warning signs [14].

6.4 BLOCKCHAIN IN CYBERSECURITY

Blockchain was initially developed to facilitate decentralized money transfers, bypassing intermediaries and preserving the trust traditionally provided by banks. Beneath this primary use case and subsequent applications developed over the past decade lie technical concepts with clear affinities to the realm of cybersecurity. The commonly accepted criteria for information sensitivity are encapsulated in the CIA triad [15].

6.4.1 Confidentiality

Blockchain, whether public or private, is constructed upon an open architecture and relies on peer-to-peer (P2P) sharing protocols. Transactions conducted within blockchain networks are public to facilitate verification by consensus. However, the initiation of new transactions remains restricted to the sole owner of the wallet. This access control is underpinned by proven asymmetric encryption algorithms (public keys/private keys), ensuring a high level of confidentiality. To maintain restricted access to data that necessitates confidentiality, the simplest approach is to deploy a private blockchain or a hybrid blockchain with authorized access on a public blockchain. Within these setups, data and user groups can be formed, enabling the implementation of information access rights based on a role-based access control (RBAC) model. However, such access management is not inherently present in public blockchains. It may be achieved through additional protocols like zero knowledge proof (ZKP) or via dedicated frameworks such as Pantheon for Ethereum or BESU for Hyperledger.

6.4.2 Integrity

By definition, blockchain confers an immutable nature upon data: any transaction conducted within a blockchain is stored irreversibly. Once recorded, this information cannot be deleted; while amendments are possible, the history and trace of modifications are retained indefinitely. The consensus mechanism of blockchain ensures that any attempt to retrospectively alter data would be promptly detected by all participants in the network, thereby invalidating such attempts. This integrity is grounded in the digital signatures of hash functions, is deemed unalterable, and thus ensures the absolute integrity of the data.

6.4.3 Availability

The blockchain functions as a decentralized network of nodes interconnected in a mesh structure, operating on the P2P model. In this model, each participant in the blockchain hosts, receives, and transmits all or portions of the data to other participants. The absence of centralization or single points of failure ensures the network's resilience, even if certain segments become unavailable or isolated. The robustness of this network ensures reliable access to data, their persistence, and protection against both disruptions and DDoS attacks. In essence, data stored on a blockchain is highly available.

6.4.4 Traceability

Traceability is one of the fundamental pillars of blockchain: all data can and must be traced to be validated according to the rules of consensus. Each transaction can be tracked, and its history traced to reconstruct the state of an account or any data. Applied to business use cases, this traceability ensures the validity of any corporate asset present on a blockchain: product data, customer data, process data.

6.4.5 Other criteria of cybersecurity

In addition to these fundamental benefits in terms of cybersecurity, blockchain provides many other specific solutions [16].

6.4.5.1 Fight against fraud

Any transaction within a blockchain requires to be validated by the network following the rules of consensus, before being formally integrated. The difficulty of validating the protocol can be adjusted depending on the security that we wish to guarantee to the data. Malicious behavior that does not follow consensus rules can easily be identified as such, intercepted, and not broadcast to the rest of the network. Public blockchains offer validation protocols that are often long and complex, while a private blockchain between trusted actors can afford to lower this level of complexity for the benefit of validation speed. Whatever the protocol adopted, transactions stored on a blockchain benefit from protocol validation, and therefore from implicit certification favorable to the fight against fraud.

6.4.5.2 Decentralized key infrastructure

In cybersecurity, data encryption relies on keys. Traditionally, the storage of these keys has been managed by central authorities—trusted organizations responsible for securely storing and distributing keys and certificates within public key infrastructures (PKI). The centralized nature of these organizations creates dependence on private or state intermediaries who are not always chosen and who impose their trust on the rest of the network. This centralization also creates ideal conditions for MitM type attacks: ARP spoofing, IP spoofing, DNS spoofing, and HTTPS spoofing are all exploitable methods to pose as a Certifying Authority and issue certificates corrupted keys or certificates. This single point of failure (SPOF) can be addressed by an alternative decentralized approach: decentralized public key infrastructure (DPKI). The keys are then stored in a decentralized blockchain that solves the SPOF of traditional PKI centralized schemes. Blockchain provides high availability of these keys and certificates, and also offers more security against MitM attacks.

6.4.5.3 Identity and access management

IAM is one of the pillars of cybersecurity. IAM tools and solutions are based on centralized architectures which effectively expose a SPOF. This model is vulnerable to MitM type data interception and manipulation attacks. We also see the emergence of certain distrust among users to transfer their personal information to central or federated organizations. Decentralized alternatives are emerging to resolve these vulnerabilities and mistrust: decentralized sovereign identity, supported by a blockchain, where the user remains the sole owner of their digital identities and grants or revokes access rights to their information as they wish.

6.4.5.4 Digital voting

Digital voting is one of the ideal use cases for blockchain: each person can vote individually via an application and using their private key, without having to go through a central organization, and without having to travel. Trust is guaranteed by an automated smart contract that ensures the uniqueness of votes and then automatically counts the results, without intervention or validation from a third-party organization. Blockchain provides confidentiality of voting, security, and transparency of results.

6.5 CONCLUSION

This chapter has highlighted the promising synergies between artificial intelligence (AI), the Internet of Things (IoT), and blockchain to strengthen cybersecurity defenses. AI stands out for its ability to detect and respond to threats in real-time through machine learning algorithms, offering proactive and adaptable protection against cyberattacks. Despite the increased vulnerabilities associated with the proliferation of connected devices, IoT demonstrates considerable potential for data collection and proactive monitoring, enabling early detection of anomalies and intrusions. The synergy between these advanced technologies opens up promising prospects for more robust and adaptable cybersecurity. By leveraging the complementary strengths of AI, IoT, and blockchain, it is possible to create a secure digital environment capable of addressing current and future challenges.

REFERENCES

[1] M. Ouaissa, and M. Ouaissa, "Cyber security issues for IoT based smart grid infrastructure," IOP Conference Series: Materials Science and Engineering, vol. 937, no. 1, 2020, p. 012001.

[2] N. Wirkuttis, and H. Klein, "Artificial intelligence in cybersecurity," Cyber, Intelligence, and Security, vol. 1, no. 1, 2017, pp. 103–119.

[3] S. Lee, and S. Kim, "Blockchain as a cyber defense: Opportunities, applications, and challenges," IEEE Access, vol. 10, 2021, pp. 2602–2618.

[4] R. Kaur, D. Gabrijelčič, and T. Klobučar, "Artificial intelligence for cybersecurity: Literature review and future research directions," Information Fusion, 2023, p. 101804.

[5] N. Mohamed, "Current trends in AI and ML for cybersecurity: A state-of-the-art survey," Cogent Engineering, vol. 10, no. 2, 2023, p. 2272358.

[6] Z. Boulouard, M. Ouaissa, M. Ouaissa, M. Krichen, M. Almutiq, and K. Gasmi, "Detecting hateful and offensive speech in Arabic social media using transfer learning," Applied Sciences, vol. 12, no. 24, 2022, p. 12823.

[7] I. Jada, and T. O. Mayayise, "The impact of artificial intelligence on organisational cyber security: An outcome of a systematic literature review," Data and Information Management, 2023, p. 100063.

[8] M. Ouaissa, A. Rhattoy, and I. Chana, "New security level of authentication and key agreement protocol for the IoT on LTE mobile networks," In 2018 6th International Conference on Wireless Networks and Mobile Communications (WINCOM), pp. 1–6. New York: IEEE, 2018.

[9] O. O. Amoo, F. Osasona, A. Atadoga, B. S. Ayinla, O. A. Farayola, and T. O. Abrahams, "Cybersecurity threats in the age of IoT: A review of protective measures," International Journal of Science and Research Archive, vol. 11, no. 1, 2024, pp. 1304–1310.

[10] M. Ouaissa, M. Ouaissa, M. Houmer, S. El Hamdani, and Z. Boulouard, "A secure vehicle to everything (v2x) communication model for intelligent transportation system," In Computational Intelligence in Recent Communication Networks. Cham: Springer International Publishing, 2022, pp. 83–102.

[11] T. S. AlSalem, M. A. Almaiah, and A. Lutfi, "Cybersecurity risk analysis in the IoT: A systematic review," Electronics, vol. 12, no. 18, 2023, p. 3958.

[12] H. Heriadi, and G. C. Pamuji, "Cyber security in IoT communication (Internet of Things) on smart home," IOP Conference Series: Materials Science and Engineering, vol. 879, no. 1, 2020, p. 012043.

[13] R. Chataut, A. Phoummalayvane, and R. Akl, "Unleashing the power of IoT: A comprehensive review of IoT applications and future prospects in healthcare, agriculture, smart homes, smart cities, and Industry 4.0," Sensors, vol. 23, no. 16, 2023, p. 7194.

[14] A. Sadeghi-Niaraki, "Internet of Thing (IoT) review of review: Bibliometric overview since its foundation," Future Generation Computer Systems, vol. 143, 2023, pp. 361–377.

[15] R. Prakash, V. S. Anoop, and S. Asharaf, "Blockchain technology for cybersecurity: A text mining literature analysis," International Journal of Information Management Data Insights, vol. 2, no. 2, 2022, p. 100112.

[16] R. Alajlan, N. Alhumam, and M. Frikha, "Cybersecurity for blockchain-based IoT systems: A review," Applied Sciences, vol. 13, no. 13, 2023, p. 7432.

Index

Printed in the United States
by Baker & Taylor Publisher Services